D0783966

Elena Russell was born in 1950. She was educated at
Moscow University and came to Britain in 1977. She has
worked as a freelance journalist for the BBC World Service.

THE GOLDEN EDGE

GROWING UP IN RUSSIAN ALASKA

★

ELENA RUSSELL

JONATHAN CAPE
LONDON

First published 1995

1 3 5 7 9 10 8 6 4 2

© Elena Russell 1995

Elena Russell has asserted her right
under the Copyright, Designs and Patents Act, 1988
to be identified as the author of this work

First published in the United Kingdom in 1995 by
Jonathan Cape
Random House, 20 Vauxhall Bridge Road, London SW1V 2SA

Random House Australia (Pty) Limited
20 Alfred Street, Milsons Point, Sydney,
New South Wales 2061, Australia

Random House New Zealand Limited
18 Poland Road, Glenfield,
Auckland 10, New Zealand

Random House South Africa (Pty) Limited
PO Box 337, Bergvlei, South Africa

Random House UK Limited Reg. No. 954009

A CIP catalogue record for this book
is available from the British Library

ISBN 0–224–04061–8

Papers used by Random House UK Limited are natural,
recyclable products made from wood grown in
sustainable forests. The manufacturing processes conform
to the environmental regulations of the country of origin.

Typeset by Deltatype Ltd, Ellesmere Port, Wirral
Printed in Great Britain by Mackays of Chatham plc, Chatham, Kent

to my son, Anton

'Then maybe you will understand this,' she said, leading me over to the deep freeze, and opening it. Inside was nothing but cats: stacks of perfectly preserved cats – dozens of them. It gave me an odd sensation.

'All my old friends. Gone to rest. It's just that I couldn't bear to lose them. *Completely.*'

Truman Capote
A Lamp in a Window, 1980

ONE

....

AFTER I WAS BORN my mother was stitched up with the portal vein extracted from a retired reindeer.

It was a normal delivery, conducted under mosquito nets. The tundra gnats were never very choosy, particularly as Tata had the ruddy complexion of a blood donor – something she'd been for years, always hanging on to her distinctive regalia: a metal heart couched in ecstatic bubbles. But somehow a serious infection had set in. The surgical threads kept sinking in her flesh, and the wound kept opening. Now – this rather delicate subject only merits exploration because it was important later. Some years after that summer, there was a local suicide that, my mother believed, threaded into our lives directly via her crotch. She liked to play with symbols when speaking of the past, for which, according to her, I didn't have much of an eye.

It was July 1950. She was twenty-five, married, a resident of Seimchan, a settlement on the Kolyma River, in the gold-bearing province of the Far North. Born to a Russian family from Samara, she knew as much about gold prospecting as about reindeer.

'Seimchan was nothing then. It could have been placed on a circus ring,' she recalls.

The settlement's wooden houses sat idly in the centre of a

1

broad plain rimmed with tundra hills and hillocks. There was a park (patches of larch trees and deer lichen), two food kiosks with outdoor lights spying on each other, a public bathhouse, a fire tower . . .

My mother eventually met a reindeer, and 'deer-people' – Chukchi, slit-eyed, dressed in fur.

Gently, making the best of her time, she grew fond of the place. Between pregnancies she studied geology – an intensive correspondence course that her husband, Kit, a gold prospector (the owner of state bonds and two huskies), was himself completing.

After handling gold for almost four decades my parents still operate better in words than in money.

'We laboured for love,' they say – a hard currency few would choose now.

I was their second child. Igor, my older brother, weaned on powdered milk at 50-below, started to grow crookedly when he was one year old and was sent away to the mainland (European Russia), first to Moscow.

It was from there, three years before I was born, that my mother had run away, breaking off her engagement. Her fiancé was a one-armed lieutenant, formerly a member of a tank crew. When they were introduced he excused himself for being so explicit in revealing that he'd also lost a kidney storming the Reichstag.

Tata remembers him with satisfaction: he had the fine body of an emperor's coachman, a matching voice; the stump of his amputated arm was tough as an axe haft with a distinct life of its own.

The lieutenant had supported her decision to study

languages, offering his wealth of experiences: 'Fräulein,' he shouted, sitting in Tata's communal flat, his stitched end flapping like a railway signal, 'bring me some compôte, si'l vous please . . .'

At that time there was severe food rationing, great limitations in choice of clothing and other necessities – including men.

'Women had that sort of look in their eyes,' says Tata. 'Permanently setting their sights . . .'

She was openly envied: the lieutenant loved her – her springy gait, her wily smile exhibiting strong straight teeth. His were like wire cutters, stained with tobacco and a bilious temperament. Eventually he would have nibbled her to the bone. ('I can bet my bunions on that,' my mother claims.) She broke off the engagement.

One day, she passed by a Moscow recruitment office offering employment in the distant provinces of the Far North, dragged herself along the queue and signed on.

Her fur coat, the colour of German salami, brought back by the lieutenant as a war trophy, was sold to a train conductor. That secured the top bench in a 'hard' compartment for the ten-day journey to Vladivostok.

On the third night of the trip Tata was robbed in her sleep, left with only a toothbrush and her Moscow provisions (smoked herrings and a sack of rusks), which disappeared during the next stop at a country station.

Passengers on the 'hard' benches were sympathetic: a newly wed couple bought Tata's earrings; an old woman,

3

blind from birth, chanting prayers, knitted her a multicoloured jacket that is still in reasonable shape today.

As Tata sat with her hair in borrowed rollers, a military man from a 'soft' compartment came by, saluted and offered, as gallantly as army training would allow him, his implicit protection. Officer Kuklin was travelling to the Far North – to Magadan, where he had been stationed since the beginning of the war.

'Be my guest,' he said, inviting her to his compartment.

Pressed pork tallow and garlic were his breakfast. His red face and red fists were like the tallow, greasy and porous. Assisting Tata on the matter of the robbery, Kuklin directed his helping hand straight for her breasts: '. . . Should have kept your passport in your bra . . .' Determined to keep her distance, Tata stayed most of the time in her 'hard' compartment, meeting with Kuklin only to share tea breaks until they reached Vladivostok. There she finally gave way and accepted his offer to buy her a boat ticket to Magadan.

'When I'm in trouble,' my mother said to me once, 'my brain goes numb . . .' This seems to freeze her actions so that at critical moments she doesn't undermine herself further.

However, back in the summer of 1950, it couldn't have been worse for her. Allergic to penicillin, she was sick with puerperal fever.

The local midwife, Fedor Fedorich, a practising vet on the side, did not talk to her much. Lying with her legs obediently spread she saw the top of his white starched cap poised like a question mark between her quivering knees. At first Fedor Fedorich measured the length of the wound using his little finger as a ruler but, after a week, he had to stretch out his palm in order to keep a record.

Roasted with a temperature, Tata was biding her time – she knew she would get over it: give her another day or two, just let her lie back . . . So she did, digging her nails into the bed sheets. Fedor Fedorich reacted sharply to the ripping sound of state property, in short supply.

Parading his authority, he asked old Natalia, a 'runner' for the maternity ward, to take on one of the odd jobs: milking Tata.

To avoid cross-infection my mother was not allowed to breastfeed, therefore Natalia came over to suck at her nipples. Tata was unaware then that her siphoned milk, mixed with leftovers from the kitchen, made a choice meal for the pigs living on the premises at Seimchan airport.

Most babies born to gold prospectors' families arrived in June or July – some nine months after the men returned from the tundra. To take the strain, the airport provided a makeshift maternity ward for the season. Tata had been placed in the former buffet area, all alone behind the bar counter next to a wooden sink. Under her folding bed were hidden a pre-war abacus and a row of empty bottles of American bourbon, neatly fencing in her enamel chamber-pot. The wall opposite the buffet's small window, half-obscured by a vast crystal chandelier, was covered with a faded map, glued tight to the wallpaper.

When Natalia came to perform her duty, my mother would fix her eyes on the map. Long sucks were succeeded by a few short ones, and Tata would unwittingly tune in to this almost sacred, chanting rhythm, her gaze following the

5

spindly lines crossing the map. One started from Fairbanks, Alaska, went on across the Bering Strait and over the Chukotka Peninsula, right down to Seimchan on the Kolyma River. Blue pins of foreign origin were still firmly fixed at different points of the route.

Once, Fedor Fedorich followed Tata's gaze and, to distract her, asked her a surprising question . . . Suppose she were to see a dozen King Cobra fighters or, say, Douglas bombers, landing on this very ground, behind that very window, what would she say?

'Aha . . . don't twitch your legs like that! It wasn't an invasion, they were *our* planes, bought with Kolyma gold . . . by the lump . . . Well, the Americans said it was just a routine exchange under Lend Lease . . .'

She wrinkles her forehead thinking about it now: American pilots drinking bourbon ('out of the bottle'), skipping in knee-high felt boots around the snowy airfields to get the feeling of *Russia.*

Seimchan was one of the few Soviet landing strips they were allowed to use: a runway covered with snow . . . outdoor lavatories, slaughtered reindeer, scoops of caviar . . . a wooden hut with a 'Tsarevna' garret on top – purpose-built for the mission . . . frightened Chukchi, arrested for pestering the Allies.

Russian pilots (some who survived were recently pictured in an American military journal, looking officially puissant, but otherwise blank) would then transfer the US planes to Krasnoyarsk in Siberia. From there specially trained airmen took off for the West, to the front line.

In those days Natalia used to arrange hot baths for the

boys. If you asked her, she denied there was much difference between Americans and Russians: 'Fedor or Fred, none of them has gilded balls . . .'

Despite her best efforts my mother wasn't getting better. The summer heat (35 plus, not that unusual for the area) didn't help to bring her temperature down. She found it difficult to regulate her breathing and was moved closer to the window, which was no bigger than a cat flap.

Outside swarms of gnats filled the tepid air like drifts of shaven hair blown by the wind. The pig squad kept up a steady squealing as they made their morning promenade around the airfield, rooting under the wings of the cargo planes. Having only five scheduled flights a week, the local pilots kept themselves busy by breeding pigs and chickens, nursing newborn babies or, in emergencies, handling a woman in labour.

Right on the doorstep of the control tower two women were sitting, naked to the waist, breastfeeding their babies. Nearby an old oil drum puffed out an anti-mosquito screen – the fawn smoke of a tundra barbecue: heads of freshly gathered moss, roasting away with spherical, almost hand-moulded, horse 'apples'.

The hot air set the distant, camel-humped hills trembling. As the daylight grew dimmer, the wispy white clouds twitched, beginning to evaporate. Tata now watched the runway for hours on end.

She dropped back onto the pillows, for suddenly a clawing heaviness had welled up inside her. A pungent smell whisked through the room, cramping her stomach.

'Say hello!' She heard the voice of the midwife talking to someone at the door. As Fedor Fedorich emerged he was pushing a Chukchi girl in front of him: a dark fleecy figure, dressed in fur overalls; her charcoal plaits, shiny with oil, followed her every move.

Nobody knew how old she was, a 'tundra child', already a mother herself. She must be just fourteen, guessed Fedor Fedorich, not much older than his ageing pet borzoi, for whom he organised special hunting sessions with half-dead rabbits.

From a distance the girl looked like a life-size version of a toy bear, all furry and fluffy. But to get close to her was to discover that your nose was your own worst enemy.

'Wash a Chukchi and he'll catch something from us and die,' Fedor Fedorich was lecturing the post-natal women. They informed Tata that, immediately after giving birth 'in captivity', the Chukchi girl had grabbed her own placenta as if afraid it might run loose. The midwife hadn't even blinked, letting her keep it for three days and had then assisted her in carrying out an old Chukchi ritual: the placenta was wrapped in a deerskin (together with a hefty lump of fresh meat) and buried under a larch's roots. 'The precious gift taken from the Earth, the Mother of Creation, was thus returned to Her . . .' explained Fedor Fedorich pointing his finger in a didactic manner.

He didn't mind the Chukchi girl sleeping on the bare floor with her twin babies lying in cardboard boxes under an open window. Recently she had set out on a determined hunt for brightly coloured buttons, cutting them from women's clothes to decorate her plaits and her reindeer-skin top.

'Well, say hello . . . She is Tata . . . say ta-ta . . .' insisted Fedor Fedorich, stroking the girl's head; she hardly knew any Russian. 'Say – I am Eichin . . .'

Eichin heard her name, probably the only word she understood, and, as if being accidentally whipped, reached Tata's bed in two acrobatic leaps.

You wouldn't expect this bundle of fur to hop like a doughty kangaroo, my mother remembers thinking, before Eichin quite casually plucked off her blanket and sniffed between her legs.

'*Kakume!*' she roared, setting the bourbon bottles ringing, then leaped away, increasing her speed.

'Ha . . . !' Fedor Fedorich said. 'She just wants to be friendly.'

My mother worked out that this exclamation of surprise in Chukchi (which proved to be untranslatable) was pregnant with unsavoury meanings, like the crowing of a crow calling in ill luck.

You couldn't argue with her: she *had* studied languages after all.

Later that night Tata climbed on top of the wooden bar counter and was stitched up under local anaesthetic. As she'd been promised, there was no place for embroidery: six cross stitches, no knots or loose ends. It was nothing fancy, of course, but reliable and, supposedly, waterproof. Before getting her injection Tata was offered a chance to examine the thread: it slithered around her fingers like a mating snake.

Fedor Fedorich watched her for some time, chewing at his thick asymmetrical whiskers.

'It's just a blood vessel,' he explained. 'A reindeer's . . . plucked out of the old cuckold before he was stewed. Come on, have a bite . . . see how strong it is.'

Tata sucked in her flagging stomach and preferred not to.

Fedor Fedorich frowned in annoyance, his tone turning somewhat defensive: 'Ask any Chukchi woman and she'll tell you – no general mending or fixing could go on without these beastly bits . . .

'I once darned a husky's bladder with it,' he remembered fondly. 'It was a beautiful job. I can guarantee . . .'

Told to keep her eyes open all the time and her mouth shut, Tata looked around the room and found the map on the wall. The length of waxy yellow thread left wriggling on her belly seemed weightless and translucent. It could have been a dozen dried earthworms wound together like a string of sausages. But for some reason it also bore a puzzling resemblance to one of the lines on the map: the same width and length, probably long enough to cover the distance from Seimchan to Moscow.

Six thousand kilometres, Tata thought with a sudden illumination, to sew my six stitches . . . a thousand kilometres a stitch.

TWO

....

'WELL, I LOVE your stitches,' Fedor Fedorich admitted bluntly, after telling Tata she could return home. 'If they look all right to me, Kit won't see any difference.'

He never did.

When my parents first met in 1947 on the boat sailing from Vladivostok to Magadan, Kit thought that Tata was the daughter of the military man; Officer Kuklin thought Kit would be 'better off locked up . . .'

It had been a pleasant voyage: a calm sea, undulating wind; the August sun, ripe as a melon, rested in its zenith. The last miles of the Tartar Strait were nearly covered and they'd soon be in the Okhotsk Sea.

On the boat there were lots of young people travelling to the Far North, wanting to work hard, make money, get married . . . perhaps kill a whale: they had all sorts of glorious ambitions. They were visibly hungry for life and love, and that famed dry salt fish, long and lean as a sprinter's foot, which you can't find anywhere now, but then no beer was considered worth drinking without it.

The discussions held on the high open deck were no less popular than the mass sing-songs or morning sessions of physical jerks done in strict formation. Some individuals wearing life-belts round their necks would read out poetry, each one standing on a separate oil drum. Wearing his hair and his name short (short for Nikita), Kit once climbed up too, but quickly changed his mind, feeling too close to eternity.

However, people were already gathered around. He noticed a girl who kept looking at him. She was standing next to an officer with a well-developed jaw and rugged complexion; his greying temples shone like pointed bayonets . . . Must be a strict father, Kit thought, like the one I lost, thank God . . .

My grandfather Stepan had been exploring the Urals for riches since he managed to step over the nursery threshold. It was a family tradition: once up on your hind legs – go and catch *glitter*.

Stepan, a competent prospector, planned to be laid out at the last with platinum bars weighing down his eyes. He would have been but for the Equality Decree of 1917. Like many others at that time he expected to be living like a lord, theeing and thouing to everybody, but found himself in the same shoes as a regular beggar. Stepan died a bitter old man, consumed by failure.

'Excuse me, officer.' Surprised to hear his voice trembling, Kit addressed the military man. The girl blushed and lowered her eyes, for which Kit instantly gave her high marks – he liked diffident behaviour in people. 'It's nothing personal,' he paused while the dispersing crowd clotted around him again, 'but what was Lenin's official policy about gold in 1921?'

Kit's intentions behind this seemingly arbitrary enquiry were well calculated: to spark a conversation, 'man to man', and consequently to achieve a proper introduction to the girl. His question, he believed, was timely and certainly to the officer's credit, for he looked like a thoroughbred workman who'd have Lenin's teachings on the tip of his tongue, set to talk you blind. However, Officer Kuklin failed to rise to the occasion. He coughed into one hand and with the other poked into his inside pocket.

'In 1921 I was suffering from rather bad shell-shock,' he said calmly, almost in a stage whisper. 'I couldn't see or hear . . . maybe I missed something. Why don't you fill me in?'

Watching the officer's hand that he feared was reaching for a pistol, Kit raised himself onto the oil drum.

'I quote,' he said, waiting for the seagulls flying from the neighbouring shore to pass safely over his head. 'In 1921 Lenin wrote in *Pravda*: "When our victory is universal, we shall build public conveniences out of gold in the main cities of the world." '

Holding their breath, the crowd stood transfixed as if listening to the great Leader himself.

'I'll tell you what Lenin had in mind – toilets made of nothing but gold.'

Some bystanders gave Kit reassuring whistles, and there was a ripple of applause when he stepped down. There was a moment of truce during which Officer Kuklin, not without some affectation, gunned his finger at Kit: 'I'll follow this up . . . what you're saying . . . if you've garbled one word – and I mean it, just one word – I'll track you down wherever you are . . .'

Kit couldn't move. He felt trapped in a sudden silence:

premonitions of doom spun through his mind like a ball on a roulette wheel.

'He was precise to the last comma. I've checked the original,' said Tata years later. Kit's mother Elizaveta had used that very *Pravda* article to line a little box in which she had hidden her old jewels. If they were discovered prior to the 'universal victory', Elizaveta would lay out her reasons on the spot: 'To cast lavatory pans – what else would you need these for?'

Who could have imagined then that the officer's warning would be so short-lived? Kuklin was arrested on the pier at Magadan on arrival. Neither Kit nor Tata had ever witnessed someone being arrested before. In confusion, Kit went up to Kuklin, shook his hand and naively asked for a forwarding address.

'What address? You must be mad!' Kuklin said, twitching. Leaving with the men in plain clothes, he spat out sideways: 'You should be locked up . . . not me.'

My parents were married in November 1948 after Kit had completed his first prospecting season. Working as a junior geologist with a small prospecting team, he spent five months exploring the remote areas of the Kolyma district. Tata stayed in Seimchan doing lab tests and filing for the local Expedition.

They shared one room in a wooden barrack previously used for storing building materials. Seimchan was 'quite nothing' then, and there were no plans to make it grow. In fact, its size and capacity were defined by the needs of the gold prospectors, but even then in moderate proportions.

The settlement was no more than a staging post where the Expedition staff would have temporary homes as long as the gold kept coming their way. If it didn't they would simply move on. This inefficient, hobo life in an intemperate climate lay at the bottom of a scale which never weighed enough gold.

The main street of Seimchan couldn't be easily identified. There were three streets altogether, running parallel to each other past identical wooden houses. In the outskirts huts grew haphazardly without being numbered; some could be mistaken for outside lavatories and vice versa. As kitchen gardens would elsewhere, here rubbish heaps divided one hut from another. These quarters of the settlement were occupied by people who, not being directly involved in gold prospecting, were counted as 'overheads', inevitable in any serious business. They ranged from builders, drivers and teachers to cleaners and shop-assistants. They knew their place, mixing with the main workforce only out of necessity and, partially, because of the inconveniences of everyday life. There were different queues to queue in, separate benches to sit on when watching a movie in a hut-club or washing at the public bathhouse.

My parents were friendly with two 'overheads': a doctor and the postmaster, both renting beds in a hostel that primarily housed gold prospectors. To secure his tenancy, the doctor took up extra duties, working at night as the hostel handyman; the postmaster followed his example and became quite a competitive stove-heater. As a result of such voluntary service the Expedition authorities saved an impressive sum, a healthy addition to the public funds that

15

allowed the laying-out of a football pitch in the central part of the settlement.

Some women, including Tata, complained that they needed a kindergarten or at least a playground for their children.

This got short shrift from the masculine party, who were learning the rudiments of local games: sledge races and sucking out the bone marrow of reindeer (a Chukchi delicacy).

The Expedition staff, mostly men, young and well-educated, with beards as prosperous as their ambitions, appeared to be a sort of geographical farrago.

'Other republics are represented better than Russia,' Kit wrote to his mother, back in the Urals. Elizaveta kept sending him parcels of garlic and a set of monthly instructions: 'Instead of getting married, find a decent old woman, somebody's grandmother, to cook and darn. Woollen socks aren't on sale any more these days . . .'

The average age of Seimchan's inhabitants was then twenty-five to thirty. Older men predominated among the contractors who, being always on the move, didn't count. Except for one local woman, Arina the Singer, clearly living on borrowed time, there were only potential grandmothers in the area.

Arina's house, heavily fenced in and with its shutters permanently closed, stood on a high bank of the river. Rarely seen in the settlement, Arina lived self-sufficiently: she went fishing, bred rabbits and chickens, brewed blueberry wine. She never invited anyone in; even the doctor

16

had to examine her out in the passage between the kitchen and a storeroom overpopulated with rabbits.

Carrying on with her studies, Tata planned to get back to work; she was looking for a child-minder and consulted the doctor whether Arina would be suitable.

'Oh, I don't know,' the doctor said, 'she doesn't speak, you see . . . she sings.'

He kept Arina's medical history in a separate file, an exception to the rule. There was no indication of her age, birthplace, blood group or blood pressure. The notes started with the words of a song: *The Tsar's our Father, the Lord's our God, I buried my mother – she was such a bawd . . .*

'Is she . . . ?' Tata asked, screwing her finger to her head.

'Positively not,' the doctor interrupted her, nodding his assurances. 'She is one of the Kalinkins . . . a tough family, but all of them cursed . . .'

Tata had heard about Peter Kalinkin when she first came to Seimchan. A memorial flagpole of a stripped larch tree, set up and inscribed by the man himself some fifty years before, had been accidentally pulled out and half chopped up for firewood. LEARN YOUR HISTORY BEFORE UPROOTING YOUR PAST, warned the headline on the printed leaflets that were scattered around the settlement by a local cargo plane.

Kalinkin would never have dreamed of such fame. He was 'iconised' in every house, where his short biography, launched from the sky, was thoroughly read and masticated.

According to a local librarian, who censored his life for the sake of the truth, 'Peter Kalinkin was a Russian Cossack, a

17

robust man though illiterate, who came to this land in 1893.' Inspired by his famous namesake he had nothing less than a 'Peter the Great' mission in mind ('if somewhat simplified . . .'): to unlock this vast, abandoned province, opening it up to the sea and to trade. His starting point had been the Okhotsk coast, the little River Ola. Hugging its banks, Kalinkin had beaten a pathway inland. He put his wife Anisia on a horse and dragged himself along, grinding down his heels, until, after they had travelled 400 kilometres, the Kolyma River stopped them short.

Before Peter's Path it was possible to reach Kolyma only by crossing the northern parts of Siberia, through Yakutsk-Verkhoyansk: *'One year long it was, three thousand versts all told, Beastly cold it was – and such beasts to behold . . .'*

These were the folk verses that ended the leaflets' eulogy in a rather abrupt manner, nevertheless obeying the timeless rules of suspense writing.

Everyone was expecting a sequel covering the rest of Kalinkin's life. However, it was never issued – a sad omission that to this day had not been rectified.

Some explanation, speculative to that matter, could be drawn from the following events . . .

Arina's house was repeatedly set on fire – it started to burn for no apparent reason and stopped as if directed by some mysterious word or order. The old woman was advised to move out after one of these flare-ups, but she said it would make no difference: the *spirits* had got her for sure, between the beetle and the block . . .

Making it her own responsibility, Arina believed she was

fiighting against relentless forces that had afflicted the Kalinkin family ever since they 'discovered' Kolyma.

Her fears were partly revealed during the last fire when the Seimchan militiaman managed to note down her testimony: *'Peter was cursed for starting the fairs, drunken or sober he laid in his wares, rolling in riches . . . Many people threaded after him, nothing to fear . . . Peter's Path became so wide – a hundred great reindeer could pass side by side . . . and at Christmas every last tribe came together: those who settled and prowled about – the Tungus, Yakut and Chukchi, Russians from Siberia – the convicts, good hunters and fishermen too . . . All waited for the traders, Tsar's merchants, the bigwigs and small . . . Tobacco was dear and for the rifle you paid with ermines as many as you could hold . . . the spirit was the price of gold, but there – there was no gold at hand . . . the shamans went dancing . . . the tambourines rattling: When the Sun cries it hides its tears deep in the earth . . . Don't dare to look for them or you'd end in smoke . . . you would, you would . . .'*

Arina died from emphysema a month after my mother had visited her, bringing me to show her – a bundle of camel-wool blankets that set Arina's dogs howling. Tata asked her to help look after me but had left with no answer.

In January the Polar Star, clearly seen, stalked the night like a one-eyed cat. The Northern Lights displayed demonic fireworks, falling across an endless snowy-white screen. It was the perfect time for any magic wish to come true.

Arina's last requests, concluding her medical history,

were plain and straightforward: her house was to be burned and she was to be buried in its ashes. While consultations were proceeding as to whether or not to recognise Arina's will at all, the floor in her house started glimmering from below as if insulated with layers of fireflies.

Under the supervision of the militiaman, armed with a fire hose and a revolver, two corner boards were being carefully lifted up when, according to various independent sources, 'the *true* face of Arina appeared glaring out from the mirror of darkness . . .'

Arina might have lived in fear, but could have easily bribed any spirit or appropriate imp if she hadn't been exceptionally possessive. That would have also explained her imaginative talent for keeping some of her belongings in a certain style: gold-bearing rocks, the size of small meteor-ites, filled five linen pillowcases . . . Tsarist silver coins bunged up a voluminous church bell which, standing upturned, pressed down piles of tanned leather sprinkled with American silver dollars.

The team of experts that arrived from Moscow to set up an inquiry, seemed no better than pirates carrying off a rich haul. They were cautious not to disclose their find, so as to avoid any sensational drama. The money was counted, packed and sent in a special convoy to an unknown destination. The contents of one sack, a bundle of candles and a tin of dried potatoes, were tested on the spot, proving to be not only of excellent quality, but also of historical importance. These were American goods delivered to the Chukotka ports by ships chartered from the 'Big Neighbour' in the mid-Twenties.

As for Arina's gold, it was heavy in weight but of little value. Too soft, too sandy, this 'dental gold' was probably the very first prospected in Kolyma by incompetent individuals at a time when the country was preparing to break with the past and enter an uncharted age of existence. There were other priorities than gold to consider. The Americans, of course, had no such dilemmas and, seizing the right moment, some of them crossed the Bering Strait to the Chukotka Peninsula in search of a new Klondike.

But it was not to be *yet*, and in the circumstances, a repetition of a gold rush was unlikely to happen. Only in 1928 was the first state expedition organised to probe the region, to 'stir up' Kolyma's golden swamps. The results were positive, good enough to cock a snook at the 'Big Neighbour' and the rest of the world. This turned out to be just the beginning, leading to a series of discoveries, each one outshining the other.

Kolyma's gold made the prospectors, if not rich then very choosy. In fact, the layers bearing less than perfect gold (similar to Arina's) were registered formally but left untouched, perhaps to mature in step with the revolution itself.

Nevertheless, five pillowcases – one for each expert to carry as hand luggage – were taken to Moscow. The Ministry, they said, was short of souvenirs.

In the middle of winter the temperature dropped below −50C. The steel pipes pumping fresh water from the river cracked like sugar candy. My parents' water-carrier, whose vodka-induced hiccups lasted all year round, took a month's leave, giving himself up entirely to drinking.

Kit would usually rise at five in the morning – to feed the stove and the two huskies, Jack and Old London, to meet my wet nurse who fed me, to see her back home. He would prepare breakfast (buckwheat porridge and a dry-milk beverage), then doze for ten minutes before going off to work.

Tata got up at nine: she plucked her eyebrows, refilled the stove, let out the dogs, changed and dressed me, curled her hair on a hot bread-knife and went out to collect snow. Used for drinking and washing, the best snow, clean, dry and crusty, came from the banks of the Kolyma River. Tata kept her snow nests all to herself, seeing off anyone (particularly 'overheads') who dared to enter her domain.

I would be left in the militia office, where the young aide watched me with the unreserved intensity of a prison warder admitting for the first time a mass-murderer.

A new zinc basin (a present from Grandmother to mark my birth) was got ready for the road – bandaged to skis and pulled by a rope. Every ten minutes Tata would stop and run round the basin, tapping her feet, clapping her hands. It *was* cold: the livid mist beheaded the trees, trapped the thick air, sharp as ice-needles. The sky went missing, confusing the stealthy wind which crept along the ground. The stillness of the river was stark – it made Tata's watch tick like a drumbeat. She cut the snow with a saw – cubes or triangles (depending on her mood) – packed them neatly into the basin and went back to the settlement.

One morning, when she called at my wet-nurse to pay with snow, the woman told her that she was quitting . . . she wanted to get pregnant again and must stop producing milk.

Slamming the door, Tata, in distress ('quite deliberately', she says now), dragged her basin right over the snow cubes stored outside the house.

She wouldn't be *used* any longer, she declared at the militia office, leaving the young aide without his fair share for looking after me. It suited him all the better: he wouldn't be available either, he shouted, and went cutting roof icicles to make his tea and to make some water for flushing the office's frozen lavatory.

The next morning Kit overslept. His hands and toes blue from cold, he was struggling in the kitchen with firewood, creaky and stiff as old bones. He gave me his thumb to chew, throwing a fur rug over my cot, when Tata, raising her voice, complained frantically: 'Let me go . . . You're hurting me . . .'

He thought she was having a bad dream and went to wake her. With her eyes closed Tata was kicking the blankets, twisting her head as if it needed to be unscrewed. Her rusty hair, twisting around the pillowcase buttons, was frozen to the wall.

'. . . She's a happy child . . . give her a rusk or this (a rubber duck) and she won't ever bother you, I promise . . .'

Israil Koshkin, the dentist, a sad little man, dressed in a white coat, held me upright like an accordion he couldn't play, listening to Tata. She was explaining to him where a nappy goes, and how to prepare a meal out of dried milk and

23

a thermos flask of hot water. He was nodding in rhythm with her words, wrinkling his nose.

In two days he was flying to Moscow for his routine vacation and also to do the teeth of his family and his family's friends. He never took any luggage with him, just his instruments and necessary medical supplies, including two litres of surgical spirit, which was, of course, illegal and therefore a well-established practice.

'Why don't you take my girl to her grandmother's . . . ?' Tata suggested, coming straight to the point and not bothering to explain that she just wasn't able to cope with a child in the present harsh conditions. Iza-the-dentist, looking tongue-tied with his Adam's apple palpitating, couldn't afford to say no for he spent his second summer holidays working with the prospecting team as a gold panner. Kit had managed to get him a special contract from the Geological Department, which allowed 'a limited number of registered individuals' to keep some leftover gold for their own use.

'We're getting along all right,' Iza telegraphed to my parents halfway through the journey.

Wet and toothless, I was playing with the rubber duck tied by a ribbon to an artificial jaw, an exemplary object set with gold and steel incisors of impressive size.

'He was drunk and smelly,' my grandma recalled when meeting us in the arrival lounge of Moscow airport, minutes before the last call for the flight to Samara.

THREE

··

I LEARNED TO READ soon after our station-master, according
to a witness's report, 'was lolling on the rail as if abed, when
a refrigerated wagon going strictly to the timetable cut him
in half'. I was then six and had been living near Samara with
my grandmother and my aunts for nearly five years. The
station-master just missed his silver wedding anniversary
which the depot authorities had planned to solemnise with
a trip for two to the mineral baths.

Those were long summer days: visiting my brother at the
Forest Sanatorium, shopping trips to the market, late talks
on the veranda, outdoor funerals . . .

Standing in front of a gravestone in the courtyard of our
neighbour, the coffin-maker, I was waiting to be called for
tea. The puffy, burnished letters of a freshly inscribed
epitaph looked to me like chocolate eclairs. Nobody seemed
to be around so I pressed my fringe backwards and licked
along the whole top line in one go.

'Have Mercy . . . Ivan the Hawk . . . peacefully . . . Loving
Wife and Children . . . sleep . . .'

My tongue clearly identified some words there – though
perhaps not in any particular order. So much for my index
finger, which had been taught to pick out and recognise
letters on street posters, yet had failed to trigger off any
genuine reading. At the time I probably didn't realise that I'd

fiinally broken free of a first-class ignorance, having no idea then of how other people cast off their own illiteracy. I did it with my tongue, anticipating the nagging consequences: '. . . A nice girl shouldn't do such things, otherwise they'll call her names and won't ever skip with her.'

I guess I liked the feeling of discovery; to make the most of it my tongue didn't hesitate in brushing across a few other plaintive inscriptions.

'What do you think you are doing?'

All in black except for her tartan slippers and a ruddy nose, the station-master's wife had come to check if her husband's gravestone was ready. The way her eyes held that 'nobody's there' expression, her question could just as well have been addressed to the flies darting at her shopping bag or the dog flirting with her skirts.

'Reading . . .' I said, bending slightly in an attempt to hide the dirty marks on my dress.

'Unmannerly child!' She hurriedly patted the dog on the head, encouraging him to bivouac under her skirt.

Pulling a dragon face behind the woman's back, I headed towards the fence bordering our garden. A distressing cry, a dog-like howling, disrupted my well-ordered march. The thought of the dog being suffocated or flattened due to his recklessness (true, in a place of his own choice) made me stop and turn, looking for a sorrowful sight.

Well, there *was* a victim there, though an unexpected one. Surrounded by gravestones, the station-master's wife was kneeling on her shopping bag – herself like a weeping statue. Tears were sluicing down her face; her stiffened hands were twisted in an impossible knot that I wouldn't volunteer to

26

undo. She had shed one of her slippers, bulbous and feather-bedded, which sent the old mongrel into a sudden ecstasy.

What was the woman's name? Luba something – Ivanovna or Petrovna? Was she crying for her lost slipper or because her husband's gravestone was not on display?

Foma, the coffin-maker, appeared at the door of the wooden hut, nails in his mouth, herring tails in his pockets. Skinning Luba with his eyes, he grimaced and spat over his shoulder – or rather behind his hump. Foma was an unmarried, twice lottery-winning hunchback. I got his unspoken message that was obviously aimed at the stationmaster's wife: Moscow doesn't believe in tears and save death till after tea, please.

Luba stopped crying. Keeping the hut door under surveillance, she planted her black-shrouded body against the edge of an upturned tombstone. Her other slipper was missing or had been taken off. When I approached her I realised that she was using it as a back-scratcher. I reckoned that she could do with a helping hand. I thought of Aunt Anastasia: every night she would scare me with a variety of pre-school stories where saintly children take refuge in 'good deeds'. In fact, these two words were among the first dozen that launched my *advanced* vocabulary.

I hovered expectantly (impatience tickling my throat like fizzy water) waiting for her to see me. She did – thrusting at me a crowbar of sausage and a goose-pimpled cucumber. Now, it would be very unmannerly indeed and simply impractical to start talking when your jaws were busy munching. Anyhow, there wasn't much to tell – merely to

27

inform her that 'Ivan the Hawk . . . sleep like a log . . .' was, incidentally, placed right behind her bottom. I imagined it was warming up nicely there: she was elbowing the sun, the sun was elbowing her.

And when the coffin-maker returned to honour the newly deceased, the two of them drank vodka, clashing their aluminium mugs, cracking boiled eggs on the station-master's stone. Meanwhile Foma let me practise: reading his chest tattoo (this time with my finger), I detected some odd, short words there that weren't worth explaining – or so my grandma later insisted.

During the winter my aunts shared the same bed; on summer nights, sticky-hot or cooling like Grandma's curds, they slept separately on the veranda. Anastasia would lie fixed in one position, latch-straight, in her folding bed. Anna, her knees pulled up to her chin, lay inside a junk trunk whose sides were full of air-holes.

They were in their late thirties: Anastasia younger and taller, Anna with her right leg shorter than her left. Both had medals for exemplary work but not a husband between them. They shared many things: bed, bad dreams, a good appetite, galoshes, me and my brother, an allergy to pigeons, a monocle – and a diary. Anastasia would sit solemnly writing in the washroom after first despatching our chamber-pots and the tailor's dummy (which she believed would mesmerise her) outside the door. Anna would read her sister's revelations some time around dawn, standing on her head doing her morning exercises. While upside down she also did crosswords and could recite the local train timetable by heart.

In those early hours the tailor's dummy, big-busted with pumpkin-shaped hips, kept her company and 'never ever talked back'. Well, what did she expect? It was headless and mortally wounded. Its stomach had once been slit with a revolutionary bayonet. Ask Grandma, she will tell you: the soldier was a real fighting cock, wearing those bullet-braces criss-crossing his chest. He'd seen the dummy half-naked, fitting a bra, the sight of which must have distracted him – at least he stopped smashing our family china, bless him. Who would think that 'Kratz Bros., Berlin' stamped on the dummy's padded buttock would provoke such demonstrative behaviour? Not only were the brothers named offensively, they were pricked thoroughly. There was then a sudden commotion on the other flank as Grandma tried to adjust the soldier's head via his ears.

Soon after that came bad news. My aunts, then a teething baby and a little 'splinter', were forced to share their Moscow flat with two other families.

Grandma's antidote for any crisis was to start life over, first thing in the morning. Her decision was to move to the Volga district, where she had been born, and have more children. This idea came to her one morning while her husband (whose hobby was collecting air bubbles trapped in old glass) was still asleep, catching a few last dreams. However, his opinion on such matters was not always taken into account.

Winter came. Their Moscow flat thrived on its communal

life: scabies moved in with the infants, the cockroaches were voracious.

'Take half a cup of potato skins, two cups of freshly ground cockroach; mix together with some of your husband's bristles and bake until crisp' was a new recipe recommended to Grandma one evening while she was queuing for provisions.

She came back home: nose an icicle and snow her only purchase. Not waiting for Grandma to take her coat off, Nanny, a peasant girl freckled from head to toe as if rolled in rusk, gave in her notice.

It's not quite clear what happened next or what became of Nanny.

The description of the past keeps on shifting, depending on who's telling it . . . in contrast to the main participants who are as fixed and unchanging as old pots on the shelf. Grandma, now over ninety, believes that somehow she has missed her elevator, the one going *up* . . .

They're all still living together in the country, not far from Samara on the Volga, where they moved from Moscow in 1920. (To secure the journey, Grandma's emerald hat-pin was exchanged for a she-goat, the same age as the revolution, which was then bartered for railway tickets.)

Over tea and preserves the arguments would soon start:

'Actually our nanny joined us later and then married a widower with five children . . .'

'No, she wasn't *our* nanny, not the peasant girl . . . we had a local woman whose brother lived in Moscow – he recommended her . . .'

'What? It was our cousin who asked me to take Vera in – oh, too tidy she was . . . shouted a lot. The Market Theatre was chasing her hair, a bull's rage sort of colour, and you know, she cut off one of her plaits and sold it. Could I trust her after that?'

Grandma's irredeemably suspicious nature would win out on many occasions, particularly when family events, those Cinderellas of history, were slipping away from someone's memory. Mine has been playing hide and seek with me since, as Anastasia said, I *somersaulted* abroad.

I would come back to see them: a grey-haired troika in identical jerseys, each with her own newspaper to read and a story to tell. They'd fight for my attention, missing their afternoon naps, walks to the forest well, chats with a postman or a wood-goblin. Chewing over the past as if it were a handful of sunflower seeds, Grandma would exercise her obsessive accuracy for details of any kind, yet still thinking in fluctuating drafts.

She went through my aunt's diary before I was trusted to read it, putting question marks in the margins. Going through the pages I found a bunch of straw-blonde hair inserted inside the oilcloth jacket. 'November 1920, Moscow' said the little tag, written in Grandma's hand. I made enquiries and came up with the story, or at least one worth considering. It was Anastasia's baby hair, the very first crop, which, if preserved, would do the same job as a horseshoe.

Nevertheless Grandma contradicted one detail.

'No, my sister Lika signed the tag. I was packing so she did the labelling. We were moving. Dear Lika – my handyman. She had fainting fits but was helping me. You try to crop two children at once with one pair of old scissors – Ah! . . . That's when that puzzling cuckoo, our nanny, said she's leaving: *Your girls are growing lousy . . . you don't even have a single decent petticoat to wear.*'

Neither did she have soap or water for washing, nor wood to burn in the stove. The last of her money went on buying kerosene.

Completing the shave, Lika had trapped the screaming girls between her legs and greased their prickly vein-stitched heads with kerosene, suffocating herself as well as the offending lice.

Grandfather, whom I never knew, wasn't around much in those days. The owner of a tawny kid-leather briefcase where a change of socks and vest were always tucked away, he hid papers and a gun under his pillow. To Lika's knowledge he kept up outer appearances, following the new model of existence without demur, but at home he would forget himself, lost in private babble.

I once asked my Great Aunt Lika about him; she didn't have much to say: 'Kostik should have married me, but he was offered to Masha. She'd been on the shelf so long, her dowry had gone off-colour . . . He studied chemistry, experimenting with photography. Masha would model for him, but when she was *too* pregnant he dressed up the dummy and used that in her place. They never asked me to help.'

Two months before Grandma's emerald hat-pin was bartered for the goat, Kostik was summoned on a military assignment to the Northern Caucasus. Before leaving, he arranged that his pay would be sent to his family while he was away.

During sleepless nights, guarding the moon and the squadron's horses, he wrote long letters home.

Kostik's dreams were frostbitten and persistent as frost: his daughters topsy-turvy in their cot, a vapour bath and Masha there with a birch besom waiting for his body to give up the ghost.

There was no mail from home. Sometimes he wrote to himself, and read the letters out loud to homesick soldiers.

Nor were his letters or money received at his Moscow address.

'What's your problem, the revolution is in danger!' the officials would say whenever Grandma enquired. She was practically penniless and decided it was time to move.

To this day she's curious about the contents of her husband's letters, which were verbally summarised, mostly in rhymes, when Kostik came back from the Caucasus.

'My husband always wanted to be remembered as a poet,' Grandma used to say. 'Of course if he had been sent to the camps for the poems he wrote, it would have meant much better prospects for all of us,' she's able to say now.

Speaking for myself, I'm glad my grandfather survived his literary phase. Moreover he marked his return to the fold by generating two more 'splinters'. One was my mother.

Anna wore long skirts and plain shoes, one with a built-in platform to comfort her shorter leg. She preferred scarves to hair, which needed more time to look after. Making neither a playbill nor a secret out of it, she abolished her underwear as an additional nonsense. She would have been happy to go naked (and tried to when nobody was at home) but thought that such impulsive behaviour could easily become another of her 'things', like Party membership or head-stands in the morning.

Her job as a pharmacist was rarely mentioned, only what came with it: rubber gloves and a white coat, an unlimited supply of sanitary cotton, and the ten kilograms of potato starch needed to keep her uniform dramatically rigid. Not being bothered by the fact that she hardly remembered her father, she followed in his footsteps and studied chemistry.

In 1942, war stopped her growing into a fine laboratory assistant. She was conscripted to work at a local military plant – twelve-hour shifts and no days off. When an overworked machine tool blew its guts out right in front of her, she counted on spending a quiet week in hospital.

Her right leg needed to be set but there was no plaster available for a so-called 'civilian' injury. She was advised to make the best of her other leg in order to make it worse for the People's Enemy. Hopping back to the conveyor belt, she was determined to keep up her daily norm.

That sounded like an opportunity to her group leader, a former pilot, now an invalid in a wheelchair, who brought newspapermen to talk to her. They asked her to pose holding some spare parts of inscrutable character and took long-distance shots. Although her name was omitted in print, she was recognised as 'as a blue-eyed shock-worker, a little screw in the rear engine, securing The Great Victory soon to come . . .'

The shifts grew longer, her leg shorter – not that she noticed it at first. When she did the thought that she

34

wouldn't be able to stand the pressures of the new production line hit her with bare knuckles. The blow was registered simultaneously in my grandmother's house. Scraping out the stove, Grandma caught sight of a reflection on a nickel-plated pot. It was like a wildly flashing torch . . . a minute passed by . . . a noose tightening, and then her feet were on the run.

She had long legs, big feet, a good strong pair for her age. She ran along the railway tracks to the factory compound, bringing the startled guards in her wake. They couldn't stop her from kicking down the warehouse door where she found her daughter sleeping on a bottom shelf which was stacked full of bomber spares.

'Little screw' was brought home in factory wrappings: a man-size overall, a funeral shade of grey and greased enough to guarantee rot-proofing. They were given to Foma, Grandma's new evacuee neighbour, in return for adjusting Anna's footwear.

His mother Galina, the undertaker, not friendly to anyone except her customers, suddenly turned out to be something of a witch-doctor with the touch of a fern and a voice like a seraphim. Nursing Anna's leg as though she had given birth to it, Galina taught her to exercise and pump up her body.

Some people commented that the two families had formed a lasting relationship – for once firmly this side of the grave.

Anna would breakfast on radio news and dried fruit, then Foma would give her a lift on his bicycle to the station. We wouldn't see her until night, limping along the wooded path leading to our house.

35

It had been built for a timber merchant whose business had been nationalised just before Grandma arrived in Samara. The merchant's wife noticed her at the station, liked her muff and Lika's fox-lined cowl, and welcomed all-female company, making no secret of her desire to have lodgers. She didn't even need to explain that a fisherman's family (who had clearly overdone their offspring) were the choice the authorities had forced on her, for Grandma clutched her hand like an orphan.

The following winter both the merchant and his wife (as well as the muff and the fox-lined cowl) disappeared, never to be heard from again.

The bedroom I shared with Grandma was on the top floor, next to the room which was our winter garden.

'Go and work up your appetite,' Anastasia would say, sending me upstairs in the mornings. The idea was for me not to play there but to sit and sniff: carrots and turnips rolled in dry earth, apples sprinkled with sawdust, herb brooms hanging on the wall.

I liked the *smelly room* best in summer when it was transformed into a rich dumping ground that would make a gypsy go green with envy. You could build a great pyramid of mattresses, fur coats, rugs and shawls and hide somewhere underneath waiting for Anastasia or Grandma to find you. They pretended they were that Little Princess, who knew pretty well what she was after. And I was that single pea who made it all real. 'Oh! I couldn't sleep a wink! I'm black and blue all over . . .' Anastasia cried in such a way that you'd regret you ever set her up.

She was the only person I knew who told stories while

asleep. She would just start talking, like the radio in the morning. On one ocasion she spilled out her latest diary entry in detail. ('Your tongue is indeed your enemy within,' Grandma used to say.)

Sharing a bed with her sister in winter, Anna complained that she was hardly getting any sleep. When I offered to change places she lit up at once, but said that Grandma might have to have her say first.

And she did, quite plainly: 'Who slept with you since you were half a baker's loaf? Who kept you warm as an egg all night, you all wet and windy?'

Despite the fact that clearly I didn't smell of rose-water, Grandma wouldn't let me go, sticking close to my side every night. Eventually she told Anna to keep out of her way.

My aunt's bedroom was a cubby-hole boxed in between the kitchen and the hall, which seemed to be specially built to fit around a feather bed heaped up with pillows and blankets. The bed was so high that if you spat in the air while lying on top you'd very likely hit the ceiling. I could never get up onto it without help, but underneath the supports there was enough space to race my first three-wheeler, wriggling round such natural obstacles as sacks of potatoes, pickled melons or jars of preserves.

The whole year this room had a concentrated smell of mothballs and a fixed temperature – one which embalms potatoes and keeps your breath visible: 'And not a degree lower . . . (here was Anna's opening phrase starting off her favourite lecture) . . . For such rosy cheeks and rising spirits – money can't buy.'

This was fine if you had no objection to shivering through

dreams with your teeth chattering . . . Maybe, I thought, the only way to keep them quiet was to hold forth all night long – which might somehow explain Anastasia's eloquence.

For breakfast, Anastasia sips boiled water while preparing a fresh fly trap of sugar and gum paper that will hang in rolls off the ceiling light. She wears her baggy *Sultana* trousers, white vest and a scarf around her waist where she stores her duties for the day. She makes knots instead of notes. Two nipple-like knots are permanently there: one represents her purse – and the other is me. I never found out which of them, left or right, works for my department as they formed a matching pair. Others, little pimples relating to all sorts of chores, I believe, formed a barrier between myself and my aunt. Even when she had nothing to do she would busy herself making a new knot rather than fuss over me.

It's entirely up to me, I was told, whether I eat a bowl of semolina or take a tablespoon of fish oil. Some children have to do both. I've met them: as a rule they grow up snotty-nosed and weepy.

While Anastasia combs my hair, checking my ears as though they are for sale, I carefully try to set aside some of her daily tasks: to unravel one or two knots I can do blindfolded before getting a slap on my hand.

On summer mornings, Grandma usually likes to do *nothing*. She helps Galina prepare wreaths, or both of them, dressed in sarafans and aprons, shred and chop anything that needs pickling or preserving for winter.

Our own kitchen is less suitable for the cooking team – a

piano's there taking up half the space. Its place, of course, is in the sitting room, but we don't really have one.

There is a room in the house twice the size of the kitchen, with windows larger than the door and a new parquet floor; however, those quarters aren't counted. Having this room, locked and never mentioned, is like living with an elephant and pretending he's not there. More than once I was smacked for peeping through the keyhole and warned that my nose would be rubbed in pepper if I did it again.

As for the room, it holds the perpetual bad odour of the first death in the family. No one has told me anything; at my age I would have made no sense out of the truth: Grandfather and his problems . . . What was it that Anna said once, something about his 'water on the brain' or him 'being in hot water'?

Closing our front door we shout a halloo towards Galina's house, registering our departure. Immediately Grandma's voice trumpets back.

Anastasia holds me and the shopping bag with one hand, with the other rubs her breast pocket where she keeps her purse. My aunt stands tall and erect ('No obstacles to her progress,' I once heard Foma remark) and her eyes play watchman as we walk through the woods: 'Mind that hedgehog – not that, it's just a rock . . . close your mouth or you'll catch a gadfly . . . Hey, meet your gypsy-friend . . .' Sevka, the stray dog living in the woods, joins us as we head towards the railway station. The path goes as it pleases, rarely keeping to a straight line. It hovers round tree stumps, cuts across a nettle-strewn meadow, then leads you into a ditch – or lands your feet right in a stirred-up ants' nest.

Behind the trees is a big sky, then detached trees towards the town. There the grass matches the colour of the pavement and all the houses are numbered, so as not to get lost.

Our house was built as a hiding-place. It is surrounded by three funnel-shaped craters – like the three warriors of folklore we always point out, despite a number of accidents (both strangers and ourselves have fallen in) that didn't unnerve us.

The coffin-maker and his mother live in an old barn, separating our house from the village and the railway station – called by everyone 'one stop from the cemetery'.

There is a market in town where Anastasia spends so much money that people must suspect we hand-print it every morning. In fact, our money comes from my parents by telegraph. They work far away and only when we're asleep.

The last time I saw them was three years ago when they came on a short holiday. My mother was giving her blood to complete strangers; my father brought me a terrifying wink-and-purr baby-doll. It lives now in the attic dressed as Father Frost, allowed to come down once a year and decorate the New Year's tree.

Maybe I look puny, or it helps being someone with off-and-on parents, but I always get a free apple or carrot or a cupful of sunflower seeds just by standing near a counter while Anastasia does her shopping. If she left me alone I'd fill her bags for nothing. Those old women in scarves and slippers, calling everyone 'little daughter' or 'sonny', would probably pummel each other in the rush to pack my hands full.

Anastasia says she won't be fooled on her own account: she smells and touches everything, distrusting her eyes. Old women wipe potatoes for her one by one, cut onions in half, worm-searching, risk poisoning when tasting mushrooms. They keep smiling, but the sparks from their metal teeth and the hiss of breath could fan a fire.

As if looking for somebody in a crowd, I start sliding towards the exit. I meet my aunt at the gate, decorated with a hammer and two bolts in place of a sickle; there our bags and money are counted, including me and my trophies.

On the bus taking us to the Forest Sanatorium, Anastasia splits her shopping in two – separating best from second-best. Anything bruised goes on my knees, the rest into a white linen sack bearing my brother's name.

Igor is my older brother, seven and a half, who speaks in rhyme, reads books, but doesn't know the size of his shoes. That's because he's never had a pair in his life, or even socks. (This is, says Grandma, a blessing in disguise as finding children's clothes makes you wish they'd stop growing.)

Igor would be better off if he didn't grow at all, as the hump on his back would stop growing too. Right now it's trapped between his shoulders and the board to which he is strapped. The board follows him everywhere: to the big window looking into the garage, then outside to the garden veranda, the washroom and back to the ward. That's about the extent of his daily cruise, made on a trolley-like iron bed, rusty and squeaking.

41

At the sanatorium, the porter is the only one among the staff who isn't wearing a white coat and knows my name. I'm not popular here walking on my *own* legs. Once they get broken or if your back decides to grow in its wicked way then people will smile and talk to you.

The other day I saw a boy, wearing a leather corset, bite a doctor who was examining him. As if nothing had happened, the doctor (his face stiffened like a pebble) rocked the boy on his knees, telling him a story.

I was sitting behind the glass door in the waiting room, bored, casually picking at a hole in my stocking. A few moments later, this same doctor rushed in, kicking the door. I froze; he hissed and poked his wounded finger right in my face.

We come to visit my brother every morning, except for weekends when it's Anna's turn. Although Igor is already washed and fed, Anastasia trusts no one. She soaps both him and his board so they float and bubble together in the tin bath. At lunch, she plays 'Open your mouth wide or I'll feed Big Grey Wolf instead', tickles his toes or cuts his nails. She kisses his bedsores, reads to him holding his hands, pretends she's been pecked on the head when solving one silly riddle of his – while I'm supposed to be an invisible addition to the waiting room.

I think I'm getting pretty good at it because nobody really gives me a second look. I usually sit in an old armchair donated by a local confectioners, think nothing much (perhaps about food) or make up my own riddles.

Igor told me confidentially that he didn't mind sharing my chicken-pox or mumps. Though that happened two years ago, the doctors consider me as some sort of sprouting bacillus. Therefore visiting hours for me are rationed: half an hour every other week, which is not really fair, for I'm fit and never seen or heard after entering the ward. So once a fortnight I tickle Igor's feet, piglet-pink, cotton-soft. You can tell straight away they haven't been used much.

Igor got sick just before I was born. He was a heavy toddler, a dozy one, they thought, because rather than crawling and playing around he was happy lying in his cot, scraping the plaster off the wall. The next thing he knew he too was covered in plaster.

Igor hands out smiles like nobody else. Just wait for the spring to come, the doctor says, and you'll be off chasing girls. I hope by then he'll lose his suit of armour. After five years' use his board must be worn out.

He has some photographs to show me: a bear gobbling up a whole tin of condensed milk, and the same bear flat on the ground at the feet of a man wearing a hat which looks like a mushroom under a veil.

I examine the pictures carefully not knowing what to say, and Igor, impatient, says, 'Don't you see – it's our papa who killed the bear . . .'

He laughs, clapping his hands, and Anastasia starts crying. She does it for no reason, so it's best to leave her alone, hunched and blowing her nose.

Late afternoon. The bus is taking us back to the station. I am sat on my aunt's lap. Breathing into my collar, she plants there her secrets: she can't swim, she is afraid of doctors . . . When I was a baby she dressed me as a boy, all in blue; if Anna took me for a walk she would deck me out in

43

red or snow-white. Strangers assumed they both had a child – a boy and a girl.

Grandma is waiting for us at home. 'Tea on the table, one leg on the road,' she says.

While we are visiting the lavatory, washing our hands, changing shoes, she tags after us asking if Igor was eating well, what his temperature was, were his cheeks pale or pink, his first words, his last words . . .

She has everything in order: her bag in her hands (containing meatballs, fried potatoes, a rum baba), money in her pocket, me sitting straight-backed chewing a poppy-seed cracknel. Thus reassured she makes a sign of the cross in the air and leaves for the sanatorium herself.

'Dance!'

Foma, whistling one of his favourite balalaika tunes, hangs over our fence. He is obviously drunk. Another funeral over and done with. This time it must have been the boiler-maker finally hammered into what Grandma reckons to be a second-hand coffin. If not (she asked herself yesterday while watering the geraniums), why bother lacquering the insides and patching up the lid.

'Dance – or I'll eat your letter alive.'

Foma's not teasing me: he's sniffing hungrily at a white envelope, which he's pulled out from under his cap.

It was the first letter I'd ever been sent, so obediently I bobbed up and down.

The letter is indeed addressed to me, my name in printed letters on the envelope. 'I saved it specially for you,' says Foma, who collects our mail from the station.

I read the letter and Foma repeats the words after me so I won't forget what I've just read.

'Papa bought you a puppy, little Mitten, but call it anything you like . . . We had a heavy snow, couldn't get out of the house . . . Are you used to wearing felt boots and galoshes? You'll need a new fur coat, perhaps *rabbit* will do . . .'

My mother also writes that she misses me.

'About time too.' Foma heaves a sigh of relief; his hump juts out like a spare head that is lying in wait.

I follow his eyes towards our house where Anastasia is washing the porch steps, with her skirt tucked up, and read the letter again. This time I understand that my mother wants me back. The puppy and galoshes are just a way of making it clear.

'When you've learned to read between the lines, then you can *really* read,' Foma says, prizing me with a smile that connects his ears. I know he is glad I am going. The other day he told Grandma if it was not for me – that 'hernia of love' – Anastasia would go whooping off with 'the man next door' right away.

He is not giving her up easily. Last night, when I caught him spying outside my aunt's bedroom, he begged me to thin the geranium jungle on the windowsill. He *had* to know, he explained, if Anastasia wears drawers or, like her older sisters, saves on laundry.

My aunt says she'd care more for a woodpecker than she does for him.

Have I repeated as much? Foma raps me firmly on the nose and shouts: 'Show her the letter, she'll pack you off before I . . .' He burps, expelling sour wind. I shed one, well, two tears in return. We turn our backs on each other, but there's nothing else to do except to make up.

I help him to roll a cigarette and he, as if inspired, suggests that I'd better swallow my fate whole by letting him chew up the letter. No, he does not want any 'thank you': easing his access to my aunt's bedroom would suit him nicely.

FOUR

....

'MATVEEV.'

A man in a suit ornamented with gold buttons introduced himself, grasping my elbow. I couldn't give him either of my hands for they were hooped around a watermelon, pig-tailed, striped in yellow.

To bring me back, my parents had sent a big silver plane and a pilot all the way to Moscow.

'He's a very good friend of ours,' wrote Tata. 'In his personal account are probably a dozen polar bears . . . Some of their fur was used to line Kit's outdoor trousers – just the thing at minus fifty. Can we have some woollen socks – the bigger the better . . . Matveev's size hasn't been on sale since he was ten.'

Perhaps in compensation for his feet, Matveev's eyes were two cherry pips – or so they seemed to me at my height on the level with his fly. He had a booming voice, to which people reacted as if being stunned by a bugle call.

Anastasia and Grandma, who had brought me to Moscow, addressed Matveev as 'Captain', remaining at a distance when talking to him.

'Captain,' began Anastasia, 'we want to know where our girl is going to be sitting.'

It could have been his answer – 'On my lap!' – or the 'Ha ha ha!' that followed that made Grandma clutch at her chest.

'Captain!' She paused, giving me one of those looks that implied that my presence was no longer desirable. 'She's not a pendant to swing in the air for twenty hours . . .'

'At the very least,' put in Anastasia hastily. 'That is if the wind's blowing in your direction.'

Matveev lifted my chin up: 'You wouldn't mind spending some time in a wheelchair, would you?'

I thought we were supposed to be flying in a plane, with me sitting next to the window watching the sun going giddy. What hadn't been mentioned was the ticket, or to speak more correctly, the absence of one, and therefore a *seat* for me. I was at that age of maximum discomfort, when I was not entitled to either of these two items on any form of transport.

I was the last one to enter the plane, on my own with the melon. Matveev promised he would flash his cabin lights if there was a spare seat for me, thus keeping my aunt and Grandma well informed about the situation. I left them hand-in-hand, growing into each other, as they watched me crossing the airfield. My cheeks and a new winter scarf knitted by Grandma were now visibly wet. I was not crying but I'd had to fight off a series of weepy kisses.

The Captain was not altogether joking about lending me his knees. It looked like he'd be more comfortable without them, for there were no seats on the plane big enough to fit him. Tacked onto the back of the passengers' salon was my seat – a wheelchair facing the toilet cubicle in a space designated for smoking.

Strapping me into the wheelchair, a stewardess told me that after the first two stops we would transfer to a bigger

48

plane with less of a crowd. As she was promising to move me up to a front seat with a proper table flap and a folding babies' cot, the loudspeakers broadcast the Captain's wishes: use the toilet facilities 'only if nothing else helps . . .' Furthermore, smoking would be particularly welcomed anywhere *but* the smoking area which, until the next landing, is considered to be inflammable.

'But I saw a child sitting back there . . .' a man from the middle row complained.

Having heard this some passengers became alarmed, jumping up to see me while we took off. The disorderly plane rose rope-dancing into the sky.

When my hearing returned I was stunned again – this time by an avalanche of offers: a chess match, a water-pistol duel, a piggy-back ride . . . I held on tight to my watermelon and, being thus preoccupied, did not have to accept or say anything.

I slept right through our first landing in Perm. We stayed on board while the plane was checked and refuelled; then there was another three hours' flying to Omsk.

During that night, or it could have been early in the morning, my legs, like a pair of woken-up puppies, dragged me out for a walk. It would be difficult to get lost, I reasoned, as there was only one gangway.

The passengers' salon seemed to be under a spell, like the Sleeping Kingdom I'd recently seen in a movie, although it hadn't accumulated such an unimaginable stock of groceries. There were no empty hands; everyone was clutching bags and boxes.

We were in another time zone, a far cry away from our railway market, but as usual I was getting my free share of loot right on the spot. I only had to mention that I wanted a drink and two bottles of lemonade unexpectedly found themselves under the wheels of my chair. A string of dried mushrooms and a litre of 'Moscow beer' came later from a military man, the owner of a portable bathtub and a slit-eyed wife. A bearded gold miner outstripped a fat builder (who'd lost his ear to Father Frost) by two to one with garlands of garlic. They were still chained around my neck when I stood outside the pilot's cabin, wondering whether a visit at this time of night would be tolerated.

'Oh hell! Do what you want, you silly fig!'

The Captain's voice ripped over the loudspeakers, causing some passengers to cease their snoring. As the door flew open, I stepped aside, avoiding a collision with Matveev who was chasing after the stewardess, his tie fanning the air. He stopped short, realising she was unlikely to go far.

'I am in trouble,' he repeated twice, as if trying out the sound of it, then patted me on the head.

'Meet me for breakfast after landing, and . . . have you brought something to play with?' He started to cradle one of his arms, but met a blank expression on my face.

For the next two days we had our meals together, listened to opera on the radio, coloured in the photos in the newspaper, organised bath sessions – all down there on the ground, stuck in one room at the pilots' hostel at Omsk airport.

With only five planes operating daily, our flight for Magadan wasn't due for 48 hours. Departure time was strictly scheduled but not always kept. It could be affected by unfavourable weather or simple bribery when some pilots would buy their way up. Matveev said, because of queue-jumping, some stranded passengers grew beards 'as long as flying carpets' before getting home. Meanwhile other unfortunates managed to get a divorce or have their teeth crowned – for these and other such troublesome services were virtually non-existent further North.

Steaming the window, I looked out onto the landing field, a narrow strip half-circled by woods in the distance. The September sky was no different from the one we'd left in Moscow. However, the trees, which I recognised, fir and pine, were shorter and much fuller in appearance, presumably already dressed for winter.

'*No*, we can't go out,' said Matveev. 'Right now I'm supposed to be in town, yes, that's what the others think . . .'

'Are we hiding?' I asked tactfully.

Matveev turned away to the wall: chin on his chest, wringing his hands. Well, at least he was sulky with me, not indifferent.

Two hours later the flight for Magadan was announced, ready to leave ahead of time. Matveev pulled me through the door, grabbing hats and coats as we went.

Sitting in the taxi, we were both putting our boots on the wrong feet. I thought, looking at him shyly, I've got so much in common with this man for whom I've saved my last Aeroflot candy . . .

We arrived at a hospital, where he left me on the first floor, saying 'Right, my girl, if that's what she wanted . . .'

A nurse stopped his reckless running: this was a women only clinic, no men allowed. But he lifted her up and, like a library ladder, set her aside.

I sat on a bench, swinging my feet, reading a wall poster: 'Celebrate your pregnancy with a healthy baby . . .'

A door opened and shut and there was that stewardess, the 'silly fig', crying in Matveev's arms. She had only a coat on over her nightie and her shoes were sticking out of his pockets as he carried her down the corridor. They passed by me heading for the exit. 'My little hare' he called her now.

A nurse pushed me after them. 'You'll have a little brother some other time,' she said promisingly, stroking the pom-pom on my hat.

'The man with the tail of a dog said, "You broke my leg, Little Red Deerskin Top. You avenged your brother, you did, who my arrow killed. So I go home to my land, to the Whip of Falling Stars. I don't take your women, they are all stolen. I take one water pan." That's what he said, then he flew off – becoming smaller and smaller, with his broken leg, his tail of a dog and the water pan. And he turned into a moon, shining white like the water pan. And that's how the moon got up there in the sky, say Chukchi. Here's what . . .'

'Who's Chukchi?' I asked.

Tata closed the book and slit her eyes with her fingers.

'The man who plays the piano?'

No, he didn't have anything to do with Little Red Deerskin Top. Renat, our neighbour, the topographer, was 'just a Tartar from Moscow'.

'Why do they have such long names?'

'Because they grow so short . . .' Tata, tucking the blanket under my chin, kept her face close to mine.

Since meeting her at Seimchan Airport when she'd embraced me so tightly that my melon split in two, I've had no appetite for kisses. Neither apparently has Tata. My nose skims over her cheek and she smiles back. Once done, I recover my breath like after taking cough mixture and forget the incident until the next time.

I sleep in a room where nobody lives. It is dark; white linen covers are draped over the chairs and a sofa, books in newspaper jackets stand behind the glass doors of a bookcase; the same pattern of oilcloth covers the table and the floor. It's like the trunk full of junk my aunts have: everything is wrapped to keep it safe.

Tata sleeps at home, in our bed-sit, one room with a piano, down the corridor. There's no place for my folding bed there.

The barrack, long as a pencil case, was built to accommodate single people, their dogs (in winter only), couples if they have a written recommendation sealed with an official stamp, and a restricted number of children.

At the far end of the corridor I once met a boy and a girl, both a head shorter than me but already in school uniforms. They stood there sniggering, then called me 'giraffe', and this friendship died in its cradle.

I might go to a prep-group at school if, the headmaster said, I get accustomed to the harsh climate and take root.

So far I've been rooting inside like a hot-house marrow. The stove in here is never out of action, hissing, crackling and spitting fire like Dragon-the-Deathless in his lair.

The land I was born to, Seimchan, is yet to be discovered,

though the view from the barracks window wouldn't make you rush. Over the road are some houses, small and square, each one attached to a personal rubbish heap, two food kiosks, a telegraph pole, an 'Apteka' booth, and, counting out their last days, twin bridges across a roadside ditch.

'We have a ski-path running right from our front door,' Tata wrote a month ago. 'Partridges are flying. I can see you skiing off all the way to the Bald Hills . . .'

'Nappies, I suppose, are a thing of the past,' were Tata's words of greeting at our reunion. She seemed to be wary about my age, hence my capabilities.

'Look at her – she's a bride-to-be . . .' Matveev was giving me a chance, but Tata held firmly to her expression of disappointment.

'She *sleeps* at night,' I heard her complaining on the communal phone. 'No, she doesn't get hysterical – I do . . . yes, she's hopelessly manageable. What?' Tata had seen me pacing in the corridor and threw the receiver down, missing its claw. 'Can you swim?' she said, her voice speaking hope.

'See this . . .' (we'd stopped in front of a bruised metal tank that stored drinking water). 'Would you mind,' Tata cautiously turned her head as if crossing a road, 'having a splash in there . . . to sort of fall in. Here's a stool . . .'

I realised she was asking a favour that might put me in touch with the fallen angels. I said that first I wanted Mitten – the puppy my father bought for me, but which I hadn't seen yet, and I wanted it *now*, not just when we moved to our own house.

'That's the *whole* point,' Tata said, rolling her eyes and

moaning like some women did at the funerals I used to attend with Grandma. No use waiting, she said, until a house drops into your lap. Radical measures had to be taken, right away.

Following me down the corridor Tata explained: how my falling into the water tank or going hysterical (it was a matter of choice) was to get us *a house*. 'A child is . . . what's the word?' She snapped her fingers. 'The Ace of Trumps . . . works better than any begging letter.' You have to prove, she said, that you are one of those undesirable children who has accidents; disturbs the hostel neighbourhood (screaming nightly at full volume); and yes, very likely terrorises newcomers (calling them 'giraffe'). And, well, causes all kinds of mix-ups in a joint tenancy.

For example, wet nappies blocking the communal kitchen sink would make you a householder over a single Arctic night – but evidently this was no longer a possibility for us.

Bewildered as I was, I promised nothing. It was new to me being prized for doing wrong. Particularly after Tata remarked, 'It's easier said than done . . .'

That night, before she read me a story, we shared the last gherkin on a rusk. I was promised I'd have my puppy any time that suited me. 'Have it tomorrow morning!' said Tata, her ears, bluish-red, glowing like candles in the dark.

Perhaps I should start calling her 'Mother' instead of Tata to spare her blushes, I thought. You kiss her, she nearly burns out. She says there's too much blood inside her, frothing; if required, it could run the central heating.

There are radiators in the barrack, pleated paper cast in iron, but with no pipes connected. The building was too old

55

to start poking through the walls, although this was only discovered after the radiators had been installed. Some of the new houses near the river have parquet floors in every room and an indoor toilet. Ever since one of these houses was featured in the local newspaper Tata has considered us as good as homeless.

On tiptoe, socks on, towel knotted round my hair, I leave the trunk room. The empty corridor quivers with the shadowy smells of a burning stove, herring and sweaty shoes.

In our bed-sit Renat the topographer is playing the piano, rehearsing for the 'concert of the year'. In two weeks the men will return from the tundra, shave their beards off, thwack each other with birch twigs in the public bathhouse and hold a big party: lots of telegrams, a huge bonfire, gun shooting at icicles and the Milky Way.

Kit might be asked to make a speech, for he has discovered a new gold seam when inspecting an abandoned bears' den. I'm going to ask him what he was doing there in the first place.

Half-full, the water tank receives me inside without a splash. The ladle, an old army mess-tin, stares up at me from the bottom as if a moon had drowned in its own reflection. Bending my knees I find myself floating but feel I'm flying – to the very end proposed: a house, ski-path running to the Bald Hills, Mitten chasing his own tail . . .

My belly-button pops in and out of the water.

If I ever mentioned that I lived in Glafira's House (named after its last occupant, a woman who was poisoned by charcoal fumes) people would instantly recognise me as 'that drowned child'. They'd tell me what I must have been through – authoritatively, as the story was covered in the regional newspaper. I've read the article myself:

'Due to the recent accident at hostel N, we must introduce safety measures for the use of domestic water tanks. Properly secured lids should be installed on every storage vessel to avoid human, and possibly animal, loss of life. Look out for an experimental scheme next week.'

Almost a year has passed since our water-carrier, a vodka veteran, nearly drowned me by pouring gallons of icy water on my head.

As usual that morning he had driven his cistern right up to the barracks window. Whistling a cavalry march he pushed the hose though and fed its end into the water tank without bothering to look inside. The pressure of the jet sent me up like a signal flare and then back to the bottom face down.

The water-carrier swore to be sober for the rest of his life the moment he saw the hose trapped between a child's legs, floating heels up. He dragged me out 'professionally', as he said, by the hair, leaving me with permanently loose skin on the top of my head.

It was a multi-action experience: I remember dozing away, bobbing in the water, when something blew me up, plunged me down, then up again.

I was taken to hospital, where Tata warned the doctor that, if he didn't let her look after this 'belching sprat', then she would never bottle a drop of her blood again.

We slept together in the intensive care bed, both sides of

which were screened by flaps of nylon net. I remember her lying there smelling of 'Red Moscow' perfume, crying into my pillow.

'Will we get our house now?' I asked, waking up at dawn.

She pursed her lips and, looking at me fixedly, turned bright red.

'You missed my point,' she said some years later. 'Nobody asked you to get yourself drowned. The idea was to make a little drama with great consequences. You were supposed to be an unfortunate waif – a hostel child who, while searching for her own playground, lives through harrowing ordeals. Couldn't you at least give a squeak before sinking? Normally people are not happy to let themselves die . . .'

By then I knew the word 'scenario' but it was too late to remonstrate with her for not telling me the full plot at the time.

For most of that first winter in Seimchan I was kept indoors and only occasionally allowed outside when the temperature stabilised at around minus 35.

Kit came home in October. A hairy man in hairy clothes. He asked me to cut his beard so that I'd get close to him.

On New Year's Eve I collected presents and news: Tata was pregnant; my brother, Grandma wrote, had started walking, on crutches, wearing a leather corset over his chest. He was expected to be discharged the following summer.

The Expedition authorities were kept informed about the changing shape of our family for, as Tata said, she had 'needled' herself into the director's office. A secretary who loved handmade jumpers spotted Tata's original knitwear, a ski hat imitating the colours of the Northern Lights, and offered an exchange of services.

'You now have to consider *three* unfortunate kids stuck in the same boat,' the secretary said casually to the director one Monday morning, while giving him his usual: coffee with brandy and a tray of unsettled questions. 'You know the family . . . that kid who's already survived a scandal of regional importance . . .'

The director, an old man from the Caucasus with a samovar face, puffed-up and smoke-blackened, interrupted her, pensively cracking his fingers: 'How old is the kid?'

'I'm not sure, she must be eight now . . . wears a pony-tail . . .'

'No, I'm asking how old is Kit?'

The director actually called anyone a 'kid' who wasn't born a twin to the October Revolution. His secretary Alla Dulina (fish-eyed, hair bound into a plait thin as a wrung-out stocking) replayed the conversation in our hostel communal kitchen.

'And I said – I'll get his file to check, or let me guess . . . Tata his wife is *my* age, so Kit must be older, say thirty, thirty-three . . .'

Four women in aprons ranged round the stove cackled away into their respective saucepans, for everyone knew that Dulina had a daughter (born out of wedlock and living somewhere on the mainland), twice a divorcee.

'. . . and *he* said,' Dulina carried on, ' "This kid has been the leader of the prospecting team since he was – what?

Twenty-something . . . the youngest in my time. And these fancy minerals just stick to his soles wherever he treads." Then I said did he remember our annual masked ball, and how last year Kit got first prize – dressed up as gutta-percha in gold? "Yes," he said, "in a social sphere Kit is quite exemplary . . . and he obviously likes children. I've got five myself, you know, four as good as icons and one bald-headed . . ." '

The director, according to Alla Dulina, seemed to go off into a dream for a moment, then ordered more of his usual (minus coffee), picked up the papers from the tray and passed them over his shoulder saying: 'Gogol-mogol . . . give the kid a house.'

As though on command the stove women blew their noses heartily into their aprons, except for Dulina. She swallowed it. Before she finished, Tata was hanging on her neck. That improvised intimacy neither of them found too comfortable.

Leaving the kitchen, Dulina searched through her pockets and beckoned me over.

'Don't play with it,' she said, handing me a little silver key, 'there's no spares.'

I held the key up to the light; it gave a sharp twinkle, doubling the room's illumination. The women held their breath as if afraid to startle their lifelong dream resting in the hand of a stranger.

'Cunning bitch!' someone hissed after the departing Dulina. One of the women, an unmarried house-painter, assiduously eyed the key's tag. 'Look . . . *Klubnaya Street, number one, back door* . . .' she read out, mimicking Dulina's voice to perfection. 'That's Glafira's house to you . . .'

She caught Tata's immediate reaction of disappointment. 'We've decorated it twice since Glafira smoked herself black . . . but still not a soul wants to move in there.'

'I knew something was wrong . . . Oh, I could feel it in my stomach,' Tata wailed, blinking like an owl.

Somebody's saucepan left on the stove spread the smell of burning hot-pot concentrate.

Next morning Kit and I scooped the snow off the path leading to the back door of Klubnaya No. 1 before the Expedition's lorry came to deliver our belongings.

I had my own room with two windows up to the ceiling, looking out on the kitchen garden. Tata and Kit slept in a smaller room; the kitchen, living room, and another bedroom were between us, dividing the house into two uncoordinated parts.

A few days later Tata sent a telegram to 'one stop before the cemetery', informing Grandma that she considered my brother's discharge premature and couldn't have him here without proper medical back-up. Then she packed her emergency bag: a nightdress, a towel, socks and slippers – and went off to the Seimchan hospital, admitting herself for, in her own words, 'voluntary purging'.

'It was a drinking accident,' she said to the woman who came to look after me during her three days' absence. 'A champagne baby, you know, not meant to be!'

Glafira's house stood in the backyard of Seimchan's park, close to my parents' office. Kit said that from his window he could see me licking the icicles growing on the fence round our kitchen garden, instead of doing my homework.

Our house had two front entrances, but we used the back door. The centre of the house was the stove, with the rooms arranged round it so that each one got its heat. The roof was embellished with a delicate chimney in the shape of a fruit basket and a rooster the size of a harp.

I have a photograph of me saddled on the rooster, watching the horizon darkening under a veil of mosquitoes. A short way off stood my parents' office; further down could be seen the gates of the park. These were the places in the area I was allowed to go on my own. Only absolute necessity would permit me to go beyond the border. 'Oh, well,' Tata would say. 'Go and fetch your ice-cream – but not a step further.'

Twice in the first two years of living with my parents I secretly visited Matveev, running to the airport and back along the river path. I knew when to catch him: he would still be reporting the 'air news' while I was heading for the radio hut.

He called me 'Kokosha', from the name of a little crocodile in a popular children's story, and promised to get me a proper sledge to harness my dog to.

By then Mitten had grown into a beautiful German Shepherd who'd adopted me as his favourite toy bone. He wouldn't miss a chance to knock me over, tenderly gnawing and smearing me in a gravy of saliva. We spent most of my after-school hours together, getting bored with the restrictions on our movement, especially during the winter. Other kids would go off to the Kolyma River to skate or ski until late, but I was told to stay inside and practise at the piano.

While playing scales I would prop a volume of *The Great Soviet Encyclopaedia* on the music stand. It told me about 'The Animal Kingdom of the Far North', illustrating the discovery of a baby mammoth, swaddled in ice near the banks of the Kolyma River.

Once, spirited by the unhampered design of our house, I painted the rooster on the roof a bitter green, which made him look like a gigantic pea-sausage taking wing. Kit then locked the exit to the roof, my deserted tropical island, where I could be a castaway every other afternoon.

That winter the school's New Year's concert had as its theme 'Children of Fighting Cuba – round-dance with us!'

I came forward and offered to sing Lenski's aria from *Eugene Onegin* – 'Where, where have you gone, my golden days of youth?', accompanying myself.

Ludmila Osipovna, our class teacher, drank a whole mug of cold water, seeming to magnify me through her thick glasses, then phoned Tata for an explanation.

'And what have you been planning now?'

Tata walked into my room wearing a nightdress, her hair in rollers.

I was reading in bed.

'They say,' I mumbled, 'that it's possible to incubate real chicks in an ordinary shoe box with a table lamp inside. They say . . .'

'They say,' Tata pulled the book out of my hands, lengthening the pause, 'that you've not been yourself recently . . . perhaps another *drowning* spell, hmm? Or just missing that little night nurse of yours?'

Quite unawares, she'd publicly admitted to reading another person's letters.

Dutiful from afar, Anastasia urged me to practise those irrevocable *good deeds*, as well as to follow my tailor-made health routine where the *nightly enema* was top of the list.

I told my mother plainly – I was not missing anything.

What I didn't say was that this 'little night nurse' of mine had quite intentionally been flushed to oblivion during the first hour of my flight from Moscow to the North.

Seeing me with my face turned to the wall, Tata sighed – I would think with relief, though she sat at the edge of my bed for some time, tapping one foot on the floor.

'You have got to be more sociable,' she said next morning. 'Come to the soda fountain after school. I'll see you there . . .'

The office where my parents worked was a two-storey building constructed out of logs that had hardly been stripped of bark. Inside there were leather-lined doors running down both sides of the corridors, which at the crossing formed a large hall or reception area.

There I was stopped by a rifle directed at my chest; its barrel was masked by a white cloth bag, the same that Kit used for storing his 'personal' mineral samples.

'What's your killer? Lemonade or raspberry soda?' asked

the man, the owner of the rifle, sitting on a high stool near the door.

Behind him rose a wooden screen similar to a puppet theatre booth, draped with curtains and painted with red and gold stars. This was the Expedition soda fountain, doubling as a light buffet and the designated place to meet visitors. There were already some children there arranging their coats on the wall-hooks.

The watchman, who also guarded the door, practically managed the soda fountain with one hand.

While waiting to be collected, we all had a drink and a cream horn; two boys engaged themselves in a short fight and a little girl of seven, realising that she'd lost her school badge (Lenin's baby face), quietly smudged her tears.

Another girl, Toma, said to nobody in particular: 'Here's my father impersonating a tundra man . . .'

We moved our heads in the direction she was pointing – towards the red banner providing a mantle for a collapsible exhibition stand of black and white photographs.

'I'll fix you some proper lighting,' said the watchman, inviting us to have a closer look.

We shot up as if roused by the fire alarm. Being the tallest of the group I was pushed aside, stepping on the weeping girl's foot. But she seemed to be distracted enough not to react immediately.

Our faces were brightened by the glow of glossy photographs framed in gold. The top row presented the richest booty from local mining: rough samples of gold or indigenous ores, each individually christened, weighed and measured. Among the Polar-Rose, Dawn of the Soviets, An Arctic

Cob, the most impressive was the Golden Calf – five kilograms in weight, posed on a silver tray. Incidentally, the sight of this immoderately radiant offering reminded me of the massive honey meringue Tata prepared for the last October Revolution Day which had exploded during the broadcast of the National Anthem.

The rest of the display comprised portraits of geologists, singly or in groups, clean-shaven, casually dressed for action 'in the field', but making sure that their metal insignia (the rewards of their labour) were in the same clear focus as the surrounding tundra. Joining the crowd, or posed separately, as a surprise flavour in the grey routine of appearances, was a Chukchi man with a suspiciously familiar face, parading his spruced-up fur clothes. In a snapshot, smiling humbly, he hid behind his clenched hands, which were held up close to the camera. Imagine those hands: monstrously hairy, with visibly bitten nails, spanning piano chords.

Prove me wrong, but these hands were playing The Dog Waltz next to mine only yesterday.

I met Toma's eyes: yes, there was no mistake. My music partner, Renat the topographer, Toma's father, was in almost every picture.

'My granny says,' Toma revealed, giving herself airs, 'focus-pocus, here comes our Tundra-man . . .'

Exchanging looks we stood puzzled: why imitate a Chukchi instead of having a real one? There were some of them around – at least ten for every hundred square kilometres of the Far North, as The Great Soviet Encyclopaedia claimed proudly.

Whatever was the reason, none of us were prepared to make an issue of it. Maybe because we already understood the attraction of being metamorphosed, if only on compulsory orders. We had all taken part in a grandiose school production of the classic Italian saga *Onions Poor, Tomatoes Rich.* To pass for vegetables, which most of us were acquainted with only in powdered form, was by common consent much more dramatic than impersonating any tiresomely irregular human beings. Actually, if it hadn't been for Toma's declaration, our unspoiled eyes would have been happy to accept anything arrayed in deerskins as being the genuine article. In fact Renat, with his high Tartar cheekbones, narrow eyes and slightly flattened nose, looked (when dressed appropriately) like the ideal Chukchi.

'Hee-hee . . . Slit-eyes! Icy bum . . .' A small, restless boy sprang up and sneered at Toma. She responded by fetching him a sharp, well-targeted blow to his jaw.

During this interruption the little girl, who by now had overcome the loss of her Lenin badge, moved up to the front.

'*Where* is focus-pocus then?' she asked emphatically but was left neglected, steaming up her thick-as-headlamps glasses, for the rest of us were busy exchanging observations:

'My mother said that Chukchi give TB to their dogs . . .'

'They speak whale language and drink deer's blood . . .'

'Chukchi hate houses, gold and vacuum cleaners – that's why they don't mix with people . . .'

'I know the first Chukchi was born to be a deer but couldn't grow any horns . . .'

Exhausted from sucking at his spent pipe, the watchman

nodded impassively to someone on the phone, then lit a roll-up and made another five raspberry sodas.

'Have you ever met a Chukchi?' he asked, bringing the drinks to us.

'I am not allowed to talk to *them*,' said the boy who'd called Toma's father 'slit-eyes', politely lowering his head.

It was known that Chukchi were visiting Seimchan at various times, almost invisibly or, in Tata's words, 'peeing round the settlement on their way to the herd camp'. Avoiding contact with outsiders as a rule, they had been seen occasionally stopping by at the airport, trading for empty petrol barrels or for fire-water – vodka.

'I met a Chukchi once,' the other boy claimed rather boastfully, the sugar candy in his cheek cracking like ice. 'We were going to the airport on the bus and he'd broken down near the road . . . His sledge was in the ditch and his dogs were going mad and he was beating them.' The boy was beginning to get carried away, then something caught his eye. 'See those two *shaggies* – they're just like the ones he had . . .' He'd switched his gaze to a picture of some prominence placed in the centre of the stand.

It captured one of the classic scenes of the northern dimension: a pair of Laikas with long wolfish muzzles trailing a group of geologists on some laborious mission. Bending under heavy packs they headed off intrepidly into the wind, towards the far-away mountains. In the background, completing the tableau, reindeer shamelessly exposed their hindquarters, leaving a lonely herdsman solidifying in the shadows.

Was it Toma's inimitable father again?

'Of course it's *him*, who else do you think? Poor Renat, he suffered nightmares after those photo sessions . . . imagined he'd be eating deer for the rest of his life.'

Tata had come up unnoticed and, pulling me by the sleeve, dragged me upstairs.

I tried to keep up with her pace and she with my unwearying questioning.

. . . Don't be silly, we couldn't have *any* Chukchi. They hate to be photographed, don't you know?

Of course, everybody here recognised Renat – he is as Chukchi as you are a red salmon . . .

And there's nothing funny about it, she reproached me, telling me to do up my laces when we reached the landing.

For a start, Chukchi have virtually no body hair, while Renat is regularly tempted to use the back of his hands as a shoe brush, Tata commented. But, in Moscow, who would know such trivial details? If the Ministry boss ever travels north he just goes butterfly hunting around his dacha. In fact, it was the Ministry of Geology that gave the order to compile the special photo album for the annual celebration of gold prospecting.

'. . . and they said: how about *polishing up* history a bit? Keep it to the true spirit, but don't go overboard – something semi-civilised. You get us a presentable Chukchi and we'll order for him some of those skin rags – a museum piece . . . and just click away. Simple.'

Tata blushed as she spoke, nodding contemptuously with each step we climbed.

We stopped at the end of a corridor, where a sorry-looking evergreen tree stood plugged into a wooden tub.

'Such a waste of oxygen . . .' Tata greeted the tree, checking if the lava-grey soil was watered. She gave it a tender-hearted blow. '*This* will sooner teem with pomegranates before you find a mouth-watering Chukchi . . .'

FIVE

UNTIL APRIL, when the rubbish heaps slowly began to melt, filling the air with their stench, I spent most afternoons at the Expedition. After school, I would pop home to have lunch with my parents, do my homework and then go socialising.

Appointed to run the Geological Fund, Tata had her own office – a separate two-room house near the main block. A minute, decidedly prim building of carousel-like prettiness, Geofund stored the classified information about mineral deposits in the area: volumes of 'golden' prose and treasure maps, a supreme collection of minerals, rocks and gold samples. A long rank of metal shelves, cemented to the floor, kept her table out of sight and away from the daylight. Wearing a pepper-black apron and book-keeper's false sleeves off the same peg, she generally occupied herself with reading.

'Pardon? Reading? I was *the* treatise editor for the entire Far North . . .' Like her mother, when sifting through the past, Tata would always be affronted by any superficial judgement.

'Do you remember my barber's razor?'

I still do: a silver-plated holder with the melancholy air of an antique. She held it vertically, bending over the scattered pages of typed manuscripts. Her two fingers gripping close to the sharp edge, she moved almost mechanically, only the quivering beads of sweat on her upper lip betraying the effort of concentration. She would scrape off the misprint or misspelling, if necessary word by word, then set it right with a dip pen: the only method of correcting known to her to this day.

These comprised the finishing touches, the last bid for perfection before the Expedition's annual jumbo-sized account of field work would be on its way to Moscow.

The prelude to that unofficial day of liberation were long winter months of collective assiduity: lab-testing selected minerals, drawing maps, preparing technical illustrations and photographs, compiling a summary of the prospecting work and drafts of specified reports.

Tata would bring work home at night to reshape some misconstrued part, 'vapid and hysterical', as she commented on these inadequate contributions, for which no one would be willing to take the blame. Joint authorship became impenetrably anonymous every time one 'science fiction' or another was found to be utterly messed up.

Worst of all would be when, in its final draft, a whole section (a veritable Gargantua of research) was publicly reproved by Ludmila Matveevna, a hairy-voiced shock worker with an unbending knee and pearl-sized warts on her neck. Never in a sitting position, she managed the Expedition typing pool. Her boisterous indignation, rarely premature or in arrears, would be divided evenly between the office directorate and the rest of the staff.

'Find me two *living* geophysicists', she bombarded Tata

down the phone, 'who spell *porhyrogenitus quartz* the same way . . .' 'Why code the map and then provide a detailed description underneath?' 'Could our lab assistants guarantee the efficacy of illiterate abbreviations?'

Answering in monosyllables Tata would take notes, which heaped up in proportion to her growing animosity. Not against Ludmila Matveevna (having once been caricatured as a dredger pump of the latest model, she then traced the artist and poured a bottle of unfrozen ink over him), but in annoyance with herself for leaving in so many inadmissible mistakes.

'How come a person of such shallow intellect does better than me? I did study for all those years to do the job, didn't I?' Tata would hail at me or at the picture of the anchorite-like academician on the wall at such moments of critical self-adjustment. I knew she was talking to nobody, expecting no reply. Trying to avoid the crossfire, I would nod silently and carry on sweeping the floor behind her chair.

To justify my daily presence in a place where others could enter only after getting a special verbal 'permit' (issued over the phone by the director himself), I had various duties to perform. There was no fixed agenda. I would either water the plants, do odd bits of rebinding or sort out mineral samples. Sometimes I felt like gold dusting, and would do it while listening to radio reports about the whale fishery or cellulose production.

'Gold can be horribly itchy,' Tata would remind me, checking that her spare rubber gloves were used accordingly. I wore them awkwardly, and gold would slip through my numbed fingers. Once, heavy ore, trapped in a multicoloured conglomerate of rock, struck my right foot and gave me a rough idea of what 'weight in gold' actually meant.

The end of the first quarter of the year was the time to tally up the work efforts of the previous season. One Monday afternoon, an oppressively grey day, the Expedition electricity kept going on and off. Editing the last chapter of the annual report, Tata realised that she'd lost a cartographer's report: a dozen maps and photographs. That's when (say just of its *own* accord) a glass tube, containing a handful of gold nuggets, toppled down from the shelf and burst. Wetting our fingers, we picked up most of these virgin metals, some as large as dried peas; but the smaller bits, of sandy texture, scattered all over the floor, powdered my head, blocked my nose, got inside Tata's bra. Under the flickering light we scraped up the obvious spots, checked far-away corners and emerged with two teaspoonfuls of coruscating mess.

'We've got some gold dust here, good for nothing . . . Do you want any?' Tata later hailed an amateur artist passing by, who was painting our film and street posters. He said it would be quite handy as he'd run out of his vivid, *triumphant* colours.

After the shower of gold, I developed a cannonade-like sneeze, noticeably more eruptive when I was on duty at Geofund. We vacuumed the room, threw away the old floor rug – the skin of a polar bear shot in the ear (one pea-nugget rolled out from its petrifying jaws), washed my hair in vinegar and dried it above an open fire. Still I didn't get any better. Tata assumed that, due to the recent accident, I was contaminated with microscopic, pollen-like gold.

'Look on the bright side,' she said, reproaching herself for yet another act of professional negligence. 'You are affected by the most noble allergen ever found . . .' Despite the fact, she added, that the gold my body was reacting to wasn't exactly of a high standard: too granular for industrial use, it was not considered worth mining after being tested. Therefore the discarded sample had already been registered as *defective*, written off as scrap, allowing Tata to put out of mind at least one of her recent shortcomings.

The rest of that very same week was less unfortunate, although it still brought some changes: our roof started to leak right above the pantry, and I got myself promoted.

At first, I suggested to Tata that I could take her business mail to the post office; then she asked me to collect some papers from the typing pool on my way back, and that's how my career as a messenger started.

For the next fortnight I was busy knocking at different doors, waiting in various corridors, running up and down the stairs, in other words, expanding my lungs and equally my horizons.

These were also the days of my growing socially *piquant*, which, as Tata observed, gradually nullified all the signs of my temperamental dullness. For my part, I think I developed an enterprising spirit, happily sharing responsibilities with people who were paid three times more (plus all kinds of extras) than their respectable mainland peers. This phenomenon was justified by the harsh climate and extreme living conditions of the Far North.

Once, when we met on business, the geophysicist Egorov spelled out what my annual income as a 'footboy' would be, were I really employed. After deducting the top level of tax for being single and childless, I imagined the sum in plain ten-rouble notes and gasped. All those notes would easily paper the whole of my bedroom, not to mention the ceiling.

'Good thinking – what else could one do with our money?' agreed Egorov and produced a box of sweets from his desk drawer. They were the finest – only a few months old – chocolate marshmallows: 'Forget-me-nots'.

Were I just another underage visitor, bored and peckish, tossing about under people's feet, I would have helped myself to quite a few. But in this circumstance, with Tata waiting for an urgent report, and Egorov shying away from it, my chances of getting gorged were very slim. Besides that, I couldn't let my professional reputation be jeopardised by some silly temptation.

So I moved up close to Egorov's table and, securing my position, firmly welded myself into the chair. He gave me a long, ice-glazed look, then seemed to forget that I was there, perusing the papers and occasionally scratching the back of his head.

There were another three tables in the room. Egorov shared his office with two geologists and a land surveyor, whom he described as 'two juvenile delinquents plus the odd number'.

His colleagues were out having a smoke break on the landing upstairs. I noticed in the far corner of the room a pair of red high-heeled shoes, thrown under the radiator, which was topped off with a curly green wig. The shelf above

Egorov's table displayed a microscope set up as if to investigate the insides of an immaculate papier-mâché heart, painted gold. It was labelled 'Rare Find, origin unknown'. The opposite wall, about a metre away from me, was taken up by an old school map: 'The Soviet Republics united by Growth', pinned all over with little passport-size photos. The Expedition personnel (some sporting artificial black eyes, others Charlie Chaplin moustaches) celebrated their geographical coming-together, marking their places of birth or abandoned homes on the mainland. This 'family tree' branched across several capitals and autonomous regions, from the Baltic to the Urals, down to the Caucasus and up to the central parts of Siberia.

I identified my parents, heads pinned up at a correct distance from each other, and established that Egorov was twin-rooted. Tata explained to me later that, although born in Odessa, he was 'married' to Leningrad. His wife worked at the Expedition lab and their two sons, my age, were looked after by her mother, a city doctor. For the sake of what was characterised as 'a normal environment gold couldn't buy', many children of the staff were forced to live apart from their parents, often against their wishes. That was 'the downside of receiving a triple salary and heavy metal dentures of your choice', as Kit loved to say, quoting the regional newspaper. Those, like me, surviving in this land of improbable temperatures and implausible resources were considered to be a privileged nuisance, whose presence most of the adults accepted with an even temper bordering on sanctity.

'Have a sweetie, girl . . . they can't wait much longer,' said

Egorov, setting the box of marshmallows on the edge of the table, in front of me.

This time I wavered. I was just consulting with my forbearing stomach which to try – one coated in withered milk chocolate or a plain, flannel pink – when the door flew open letting in a man who, though looking young, was completely bald. Walking over to his table he leisurely picked at his nose and started humming 'Ma-ma-ya-kero . . . Ma-ma-ya-kero . . .'

The two girls who followed him in were both thin and tufty-haired. The blonde one, wearing a checked shirt and tight trousers, circled behind my chair and left my standard school plait dangling without a ribbon. Quite magic, I thought. Her taller companion, with false eyelashes and pimply skin, performed a different trick. First she fanned her hands through Egorov's papers, making him shudder and bite his lip, then somehow she caused the marshmallows to disappear. The box was found shortly on top of her table with nothing else on it but a piece of oilcloth, in black and white squares.

'I told you,' Egorov frowned, jabbing his elbow into my side. 'Those two – potential inmates . . . no experience needed.'

Gazing around I realised that Mamayakero, 'the odd number', was quite openly eavesdropping.

'Hello,' he said, his eyes measuring me up and down, 'are we missing out on some intimate introductions?'

Egorov started fidgeting on his chair, watching the girls sort through the marshmallows. I wanted to leave, as I didn't like the way Mamayakero was looking at me.

'No, I mean it,' he frowned. 'Do we know you, antelope-gnu?'

Somebody (I think the pimply girl) gave out a flat, spontaneous giggle. The blonde one said phlegmatically: 'You shouldn't take her at face value.'

She sounded like she'd back me up, but I wasn't hurt anyway: you couldn't really compare 'antelope-gnu' with 'giraffe' or other nicknames I'd been awarded, which typically were four-hoofed ruminants.

Meanwhile Mamayakero had taken his chair and carried it over to the girl's table. They'd just finished setting up the marshmallows on the squares of the oilcloth: *flannel pink* opposite *withered milk*.

'It's not fair,' said Egorov above my head. 'As far as I can remember, it's my turn to play.'

At this point I realised the significance of these singular preparations: a game of draughts was ready to start.

'You can't do that to me. I *did* sign for this game,' Egorov said vociferously, pursing his lips.

'But you always win – it's boring to play with you,' protested the blonde girl, unaware that she had overdone the reproof.

'It's *boring* to squeeze pimples all day,' he retorted, managing to demonstrate that he was in effect a fairly committed worker.

'Well, guess what I see,' said the pimply girl, unabashed, subjecting Egorov's body to intense scrutiny, down to the waist where his shirt had come loose. 'Yes . . . Always got our hands full and busy, haven't we?'

79

Egorov stopped stirring his hands inside his pockets and swore.

'There is reason to believe that three of my colleagues came to blows over a box of chocolates . . . Who started it?'

I was being questioned the next morning on the flowery Caucasian rug, the insignia of authority, adorning the director's office. Vano Archilovich himself had come to the school to fetch me, stuck halfway up the climbing rope, and thus rescued me from getting a sore rump.

Behind a desk the length of a springboard, he sat over-zealously rinsing biscuits in his tea. They all went down at regular intervals (the sixth had just been consumed), but the waiting game had none of the desired effect. Not knowing what my interests were likely to be in this affair, I stumbled tactically.

The director left his seat, walked around me, trampling the rose bushes, and changed the subject. 'I first saw you when you were just this . . .' He levelled his hand at table height to make himself clear. 'So small that you managed to dive into the water tank. What is it you're up to now?'

What am I? I thought, consulting the ceiling, then heard myself asking out of the blue: 'Is your squirrel Bella going to have any babies?'

The day before I'd learned that Vano Archilovich kept a pet squirrel that was almost tame. I would have liked one for myself, ideally just a few days old, and train it to cut up sugar lumps or gnaw away at the icicles obstructing our windows.

An inscrutable smile set on the director's face.

'Who told you I had a squirrel?'

'Nobody. I just heard,' I said, budging my feet to and fro in case they'd got stuck (they hadn't).

'So what else have you heard . . . ? Possibly . . . about me – ah?'

He rubbed his hands in breathless expectation. I bounced on my feet, letting my thoughts settle. I'd rather be climbing the rope than repeat what I'd overheard yesterday about his Bella and about him personally.

'. . . One can do with one's pimples what one wants.' The blonde girl supported her friend who'd been accused of not being worth her salt. 'I might as well stand on my head if there's nothing else to do . . . It's like taking part in a yawning competition here – everybody close to dropping off. And don't tell me: it's winter, we're stuck indoors.'

Sticking to his priorities, Egorov didn't seem to be listening. 'Give me my marshies back. They're my birthday present . . .'

'Not any more,' sighed Mamayakero, staring at the draughts' formation on the oilcloth. In a second he made a quick move and took two marshmallows.

Egorov twitched and dropped the papers he'd been gathering for me, I guessed, to take back to Tata. Preparing to leave, I collided with the blonde girl, Masha, who shoved me down onto her seat, the *withered-milk* side ('Have a go,' she said), and shouldered Egorov aside. Backing her up, Ruslana couldn't wait to kick up a row: words spinning, hands winging, she took it out on everything.

If it hadn't been for gold she would have married a

tragicomic dramatist . . . well, never mind now, but she won't let the best years of her life be crossed out, just like that . . . She snapped her fingers and simplified the matter. They – the university graduates – weren't even trusted to do elementary lab work. ('Test your ear wax first . . .' was the single constructive suggestion that had come along); the hostel where they lived was no better than a cave, the local shops sold Stone Age goods, badly imitated . . . There was nowhere to go out to – the cinema club showed prehistoric films, the only restaurant (overlooking what? yes, exactly – a football pitch) served semolina porridge flavoured with herring oil, and flattened footballs filled the rest of the menu. And where, ah, was all that well-publicised scenery of peripheral merit – the Northern Lights and sublunar mirages, the solar wind and flares. . .?

She paused, presumably to make a fresh start, when Egorov, wrought up, seized his chance. He pitied Ruslana for being so short-sighted: right under her nose the Chukchi were still leading an unconstitutional tribal life, with half a dozen wives each, and no knowledge of hygiene or table manners. And all she cared about were some sky displays and other decadent *hiccups*.

'Leave Chukchi out of my life!' bawled Ruslana, effortlessly standing up for herself. 'They are happy as they are – nothing'll change them.'

'Oh well, we'll wait and see,' Egorov hissed. 'They've learned how to drink vodka after all, so why can't they live as the rest of us do?'

The office hooter, blaring out by mistake, did not interrupt this outbreak of opinions, that was to stay in my memory.

82

For I had to reconstruct the events at least twice: by request of my parents before the Expedition director had tried to satisfy his inquisitive mind.

Incidentally both of our names soon came up (separately but connected coherently) during the same rather expansive wrangle. Mine was called out first – at the least suitable moment. Ruslana glanced at me, warming a marshmallow behind each cheek, and stated firmly: I would also grow up fat and pimpled because of getting bored too.

I thought I was having fun, considering my advantageous position in the game: Mamayakero had lost most of his marshies to me and I'd been hoarding mine. I didn't want Masha to take her seat back. I was sitting pretty. Keeping my ears pricked up and my mouth full I followed her litany of complaints. Thank God, she showed a proper spirit, speaking volumes:

'Despite the fact that we're bored all the time . . . ' she tamed her leaping breasts by crossing her arms, 'what do we constantly hear: Just wait until you get to the field, won't have a minute to spend behind the bushes . . .'

'I know what you mean,' Ruslana put in. 'I eat plants . . . and Slavka (she nodded at Mamayakero) plucked his hairs out – one by one, because he was getting torpid.'

'Well that's nothing.' Masha had that promising look and, sure enough, delivered a story about the extremes people would go to – to kill time.

Take our head, Vano Archilovich, she said, a good man and all, holding an important position, but everyone knows he spends hours in his office watching flies procreating on the ceiling. Then he goes home and the whole evening literally dunks himself in spirits of any proof or origin. And there is his Bella-pet, nimble as squirrels are, trained to have her meals at the table in the communal kitchen. His neighbours say he complains about getting scurvy every year around May Day. 'And nobody cares,' he whines, sharing Bella's pine nuts, a side dish for his drinking sessions.

Bella-pet was a good listener, not like Rosa-Mimosa, the director's wife, who had left him a few years before. 'There's no life for me here,' she wrote in a message before flying back to their native Georgia to run some rather cushy trade. Vano Archilovich would never admit (it was a sort of kick below the belt) that selling Caucasian oranges in Moscow private markets was much more profitable and yes, a very merry business compared with 'striking gold'.

Vano Archilovich would look the squirrel in the eye, beating his chest: 'That woman, I swear, didn't have a grain of patience. You know – it took God seven days to create the world . . . and she'd say: well, nobody's perfect. *He* definitely miscalculated on some parts of it.'

He'd delve further into his cup while Bella, hopping on her hind legs, waited patiently for a treat. There on the table stood a crystal sugar bowl, inside which some walnuts, large as fir cones, lay soaked in lemon vodka and tears. This was a chef's speciality (Vano Archilovich concealed the recipe), as safe or as dangerous as your mood required. Such being the case, one squirrel handful of this concoction was enough to tip Bella over on her back. She was in no state to know that her nipples, the size of a pin-head, were no longer unapproachable. At his respectable age of a working pensioner, the director was reduced to constructing a male fantasy out of the prone squirrel's belly.

'Theoretically there should be a corresponding article in law about animal molesting.' Coughing significantly, Masha finished her story. Her last word, new to me and strongly out of favour, had given me a momentary taste of ditch-water in my mouth.

That unpleasant sensation came back in force when the director, questioning me in his office, pressed his cobble-stone hand into my shoulder: 'Didn't hear anything, know nothing, well, at least you don't tell lies. People lie to me. I know what they think: the old moose has lost his horns and hoofs.' On that dreary note Vano Archilovich reverted to the subject to which we were both partial. No, *no* baby squirrels, *no* Bella-pet. She'd departed this life (his eyes rolled up instantly) a week before.

By a curious coincidence, on that very day, the director's mother had celebrated her ninetieth birthday: '. . . went horse racing in the mountains and rode over one of the judges – bad sign indeed.'

He saw me to the door. It was mere farce for I already stood one step from the threshold, having been slowly moving in that direction since I first entered the room. The Expedition's latest unprecedented conflict seemed to be left forgotten for the time being.

I pushed the door handle and the director, as if gambling on his last chance, went on asking what I was doing at Egorov's office anyway.

'Playing draughts, you say . . . quite right – keeps your mind ticking. Twenty sit-ups in addition daily and it'll make a *man* out of you . . .' With hands searching for his symbolic waist, he tried to bend his knees. They produced a piston-like cracking that followed me down the corridor.

The spring of 1960 came in unusually warm and mellow. Seimchan overflowed with thawing garbage heaps that spawned numerous noisome springs, all running through the central park. Colonies of sparrows and jackdaws gathered at the most lucrative places. Things came to a pretty pass for the homeborn flies who had difficulty pestering the heavily saturated air. When going outside, people plugged their noses with perfumed cotton or chopped cloves of garlic – as our water-carrier did; dogs kept sneezing, blowing away wisps of shedding hair.

The morning sun rose like a disc of glass fire into the vacant purple of the sky. The streaming light, bleach-white, blemished your vision with its fluorescent display. Blinking my eyes, I was watching over a flock of pigeons that occupied the Expedition roof. These were carrier pigeons, ageing, with mangy feathers. Their owner, a local builder, named them after fighting planes, mainly of World War II vintage: Migs, Yaks, B-25s, King Cobras, and Messerschmitts (two identical earth-grey doves with the wing span of an élite fighter). Overfed on tinned corn and crushed fishbones, the birds greeted the pervading spring in a half-swooning condition. With their heads drooping, they were glued to the edge of the roof, releasing an imposing quantity of grapeshot on the May Day banners that flapped below.

The golden hammer and sickle appliqué were soiled in a distasteful pattern. We'd heard indirectly that the Expedition caretaker had sent a thunderbolt-ultimatum to the builder: either your wilting gamy-birds or my revolutionary banners, steeped in the people's blood.

As is well known, responded the guilty party, doves are the symbol of peace throughout the world, including the dilapidated capitalist countries. Touch one of their harmless little feathers and you turn into a gory butcher.

Having advanced angina and a conscience nurtured by Party membership, the caretaker gave in. He washed the sacred drapes overnight and hung them up, fresh and spruce, first thing in the morning.

'If only I could get a couple of spares, I'd breathe again,' he admitted publicly at the holiday planning meeting, warning in advance that he might be forced into early retirement.

'Oh Pasha, dear pebble-head,' sighed the chief accountant, a Party veteran. 'What's wrong with you – *spare banners*? It's like asking for disposable Kremlin Stars . . . One would think you'd fallen off some Mississippi train.'

It was the troubled caretaker that I was waiting for outside the Expedition's main entrance. Around my felt boots formed an aggravating puddle of noisome water which was flowing from the courtyard. Its unlimited space was freely used for depositing dogs' mess and loads of litter, accumulated over the winter. I had come to ask if any paper, glass or metal scrap could be collected for recycling, as our school needed money to support the Cuban revolution.

Well, we were interested generally in Cuba's children and how to bring about happy developments in their (until

87

recently) misshappen childhoods. We aimed to supply the Little Island of Freedom with second-hand toys, approved and disinfected by our school nurse, folding pop-up books, easily understood in any language, albums of photographs revealing our whereabouts, local souvenirs and one thousand red Pioneer scarves, which every class was preparing at domestic economy lessons. The 'Red Thousand' were in particularly bad shape: there were financial difficulties lying ahead and not enough suitable fabric to start with. The haberdashery 'corner' of Seimchan's only Universal Stores displayed grandmother's calico and crinkled plush the colour of nappy rash.

Having heard my request, the caretaker agreed not to grudge anything for the sake of Fidel's children. 'Take whatever you like,' he said, guiding me through the litter empire.

He wished he could be more useful (considering it was such a good cause) and suggested he might endow me with a bolt of blood-red satin he'd obtained from the regional workshop producing brassières and sporting pennants. But something, perhaps my unduly famished look, made him change his mind. The way things were going outside the country, he said, *breaking* with the past might become a bad habit, like burping at the table. He apologised if such frankness offended me. He believed, and it seemed his theory wasn't spun out of thin air, that there could be dozens of 'Cuban' mix-ups in different continents every day before the morning weather broadcast. After all, the world-wide upheaval had been predicted since the last century and by *whom?* (He stumbled over some rubbish.) By no one else but better sorts of Westerners, trifling away their fortunes. Serves them right.

I halted as it occurred to me that the blood-red satin was slipping away from under my very nose. 'Beware!' The caretaker stopped all agog: his foot was trapped in a pile of half-burned paper topped with rusty cans and broken glass. 'Yes,' he carried on, 'beware of helping others – they won't be satisfied until they've ripped off your last puttee . . .

'And that reminds me,' he added, sensing my want of independence before we reached the back gate. 'Charity begins at home.'

He had a deal in mind. His banners (at least three out of five) had to be patched or darned. Being a man he was unsure about the treatment required, but one thing was certain: through constant washing they'd fallen into rags. Would our school like to do the job for a profitable reward?

Options were meagre, so I didn't rush to answer, busy calculating: *Pravda*'s full edition of the last decade or ten crates of empty champagne bottles, already washed and packed, waiting to be collected for ten roubles in return. No other junk, I knew, would be valued as highly as that, except for scrap iron, which in the area we lived didn't seem to find many takers. However, recycling *Pravda* – despite clear financial losses – would be more in line with the standards our teachers had set for us. We'd been warned: making other children happy doesn't mean spending your own childhood trotting round communal dumps.

'Personally I don't like to haggle,' said the caretaker, confronting me. He pegged his nose with two fingers and gave an energetic blow to one side. 'Particularly where Cuba is concerned.'

I mentally marked where he'd hit the target (a pyramid of untouched waste) as devalued ground.

We came to the back gate, tied to a makeshift fence of young alder trees. As I decided to stay and examine what could be harvested, the caretaker provided me with these parting words: 'Show me your litter and I'll tell you *what* you are . . .'

Precisely, I thought, live and learn. With my mouth open I stood long enough to catch a fly, while he was commenting on some very petty issues. An ordinary individual would never disclose, for example, how much he *really* drinks, but his bottles do; therefore he stows them away. Wouldn't you? 'Ah . . .' he read my expression of doubt affirmatively, 'so would I.'

With the same unnecessary firmness he laid out an offer our school couldn't refuse. If we were to do business together, he would give us a list of every local trash pile that had been intentionally hushed up and kept from public view.

Some dig for gold, others, underground litter, he said in a didactic tone, peering at the sky. 'I'll draw you a map. Ask your father how to read it.'

Preparing for the new prospecting season, Kit brought his working dog to live with us. Before that Gosha stayed with a militiaman who forgot to feed him but demanded his services, such as sniffing out lost socks or missing files of non-existent criminals.

'You don't need a map if Gosha is escorting you,' said Kit, encouraging me to wear rubber boots and gloves when raking through catacombs of personal dregs. 'And take notes of what you find and where – one day it'll return a hundredfold.'

Parents could be your worst enemies once you let them become your best friends. It was all right to sally through somebody's backyard: dogs yapping, zinc wheelbarrow full of junk, rattling like musketry in a cave, leaving behind fresh harrowings of rot. But if you were to start scribbling in the face of a fleecy, lisping wind, marking areas that had already been checked, purely to avoid confusion (besides whatever else Kit had in mind), then there would soon be some unequivocable signals sent:

'You tear up those papers of yours right now or I'll boot you out of here!'

The hollow booming voice, as if coming from the depths of the earth that my team, Toma and her sister Ira, had just ploughed up, sent us scurrying away.

'I've never seen that garbage before in my life. I don't even live here . . .'

'Then bask in the sun, why worry?' Ira the oldest among us, already wearing an adult-sized bra, murmured to herself with her usual common sense.

I couldn't help thinking that the caretaker's observations were not devoid of sense: there *were* people in our settlement, alas, with troubled consciences if they were so prone to treat their litter as skeletons in the closet. Of course for bailing out Cuba's children the substance was more important than anything less material.

91

Cutting ways to the next unseen but well-suspected personal slum we kept any other obstinate competitors in awe of our ingenuity and success. School virtually ceased to function. Our teachers, themselves competing for the kudos, could hardly wait to get us back on the road to a hundred per cent profit.

'As long as you don't sail off to Cuba or pick up cholera . . .' Tata was happy to see me return home just to have dinner and go straight to sleep. She'd got her freedom of action, knowing that I was busy and not alone (well, with my relatively safe entourage). In this case my benefit was incomparably greater. I was no longer a stranger to my surroundings and grew fond of their reserved but uncompromising face. I began to feel the presence of this land – a comfortable feeling like after being massaged with hot bear's fat.

Remembering the place I see my 'proof impressions' in strictly plain colours. This may not be decorative enough for any succulent description but it is what repeatedly comes to mind. Irrelevant to the dominant, clear-spoken simplicity of the North, 'tinted' pictures don't provoke my memory. Justifying the momentary incoherence of nature they were rarely observed: be it the luminous whiteness of a reanimated sun, distorting light and space, or tufts of spring greenery, looking too artificial for a funeral bouquet.

In those days I'd seen plenty of open vistas. What might lie behind the smaller hills, the big hills, the hills on hills, didn't matter a straw unless it could go for recycling.

SIX

··

'IGOR'S TESTICLES worry me. One is hanging lower than the other. Surely they ought to be symmetrical. And it looks to me as if they are shrinking.'

Anastasia had mixed up the envelopes, sending to me the letter intended for Tata. It had happened once before, for she would write to both of us every third Tuesday after spending the whole day out. She (and Grandma's home-made aniseed caramels) went off to town to have some fun – that is, to try to find something new, worth talking about to my brother or putting in a letter to me.

There was her morning spent in Samara's Central Library (the lecture hall in particular); afternoon hours stretched up to 7 pm – which was the end of the children's late film show. Her favourites were cartoons and old features, especially *Ali Baba and the Forty Thieves*.

She took Igor to see the movies once a week and knew what he would like best. He said he *loved* them all, but preferred Sherlock Holmes. Igor lived on books and fruit jellies, Anastasia didn't hesitate to report. As a result his eyesight suffered and already he talked like an old man lecturing everyone about life and death.

'Why?' Tata would hold Anastasia 's letter with antipathy, as if it were making faces at her. 'Why does she write such things to me? I don't want to know – always some problem.

Last month her warts started duplicating and what then – Anna walked into a butting cow?'

Tata had an appointment at the hairdresser's to have her hair and her false hair-piece dyed a 'classical' mud-red. Coming home from school, where we were helping with summer decorating for the new term, I met her on the porch poised to drop the keys into one of my rubber boots kept outdoors. The mail was left unopened, stowed away on the top step. She must have looked through the women's monthly magazine which I noticed was folded to the cookery page. It had really been Kit's magazine since he started collecting recipes.

The previous spring Kit had written to the editor-in-chief of the magazine (apparently a man) and asked him how one could pickle mushrooms without a drop of vinegar, as there was never any for sale in Seimchan. But so far, in all the issues throughout the summer, the cookery page had been concerned with preserving tropical fruit and berries found predominantly in the Mediterranean region.

Sitting on the porch rail I sorted through the rest of the mail and read Anastasia's letter, written in a childlike hand mostly in printed letters. She asked my mother's permission to order Igor a suit, tailor-made, double-breasted, with shoulder pads and a waistcoat which would help, she believed, to cover his 'structural' faults.

'He's such a handsome boy, smells of fruit jellies. You should be proud of him,' she wrote, then brought up the subject of his testicles. 'They're never the same. *Can* they shrink or is it just me imagining things?'

My aunt must have had easy access to my brother's

testicles, I thought. My ears blushed; I pleated the letter into a fan.

It was a hot afternoon, fly-bitten, camouflaged in spasmodic whirls of dust. July had ended in August, cutting short the brief autumn – a dead season lasting only a few days before the early frost which preceded the first snow – the best time of all.

The settlement stayed quiet: most of the children were still away on holidays, the men continued their field work, the women busied themselves indoors. Dogs were permanently outside, drowsy from heat. They sniffed each other's bottoms and yawned. Thanks, but no thanks . . .

Without multiplying the boredom there is not much to add to my recollections of the summer holidays of '61; hours spent watching our winter clothes being aired in the kitchen garden, or pacing the streets, powdered with dust, as empty as my head.

Twice I was asked to look after my music teacher's kids. At her house I discovered a full-length mirror, a complete edition of Maupassant and a padded bra – creamy satin, caramel buttons. As I tried it on in front of the mirror my heart gave a curt, appreciative spasm.

If only Anastasia could get herself a padded bra, it would change her life! She wore a plain one stuffed with cotton balls, which she had to roll up every morning. And she worried constantly that they'd slip down or leap up to her chin every time she moved.

'She's chronic,' Tata once said, sighing sympathetically. 'Still in her teens . . .'

It meant I was catching up with my aunt, not that I'd ever felt far behind her. Now we could carry on growing together, albeit apart, but nevertheless sharing our experiences. She was learning about testicles; I was very much into padded bras. That's what I would write to her, I thought, picking myself up from the porch. She should order herself a padded bra. And a couple for me.

As soon as I unlocked our front door, the phone started ringing. It was my mother's hairdresser – I recognised her throaty, rattling voice. She asked why I'd been sitting outside like an abandoned bride and whether there had been any calls for Tata in the last half hour. Before I had a chance to answer, she repeated my mother's words, themselves so audible I could hear them in the background: 'Don't forget to take messages . . . now, get inside . . .'

'Where do you think I *am*?' I shouted into the receiver. It swore back at me, challenging if not angry. It seemed I'd hurt the hairdresser's hearing.

Invariably hoarse with talking, this woman enjoyed briefing her clientèle on the latest news before anyone could verify it.

A fortnight before, when Tata was waiting in a queue to have a trim, the hairdresser, as usual, had gone 'on the air'.

Magadan's regional museum, she rattled on, was presently exhibiting a rare example of permafrost fauna – an Arctic water lizard, a triton. It had been found by a gold miner, hammering through unimaginably deep layers of rock. Crystallised with ice, the triton was soaked in a salad bowl to defrost and, surprisingly, was resuscitated courtesy of the central heating and an overcrowded communal dwelling.

Compact, no longer than a small pair of scissors (the hairdresser was taking it personally), the triton had a detached tail swimming fondly after its body – which was, by the most conservative calculations, a couple of thousand years old. Fed on sifted flies, this panting specimen stayed remarkably unshaken at the sight of a plastic sea turtle with a wind-up heart, brought in as a temporary companion.

'This ought to be seen . . .' Tata quickly put forward a suggestion, which was greeted with a conspiratorial bustle among the other women visiting the salon.

The night was white, with a ghostly moon, when they planned their secret weekend in Magadan – one week before the school term started. The necessary preparations were fully discussed but cut to a minimum: children to get off their hands, tickets to buy, dresses to make (no funeral colours or anything anti-mosquito) . . . Husbands to be kept in the dark.

The latter was the least difficult because there was no contact with the prospecting teams except via the radio calls, booked in advance for mutual convenience.

Ever since the trip to Magadan had been on the cards we had had no cooked meals: Tata was trying to lose weight. A thing not to be mentioned. She would frame you with a look of pure hate if you did, then go back to jumping over the stack of firewood, fighting the mortal fight against her knee flab and belly ruffles.

Waiting for my mother to come home I developed the

appetite of a boa constrictor. The kitchen cupboards gaped empty, the pantry was locked, the stove cold. Mouthing hungry looks in the hall mirror I went outside. Tata was labouring up the porch steps with shopping bags, singing 'Triton – Tritosha, Totosha . . .'

'I have to start somewhere,' Tata said, pulling me off the path.

We were doing her evening run, alongside the road ditch, trailed by a gang of children under five. They stopped too, stumbling over their horses and weather-cocks on wheels.

Tata stood motionless watching the sun drooping. She wanted changes in her life, she said, anything unplanned and off-compass. She could do with sailing to unknown destinations or dancing to a juke-box dressed in taffeta and a French beret.

'I'm nearly forty and I won't live forever,' she said, as if I would.

Tata arranged for me to stay at my music teacher's house for the time she would be visiting Triton the lizard.

We had our dinner together: rusks and raspberries in syrup (my 'cough mixture') for me and Armenian brandy for Tata. She sat, wrinkling her nose, her breasts heaving. Berries never agreed with her. She sipped brandy while checking her watch with the intensity of a bomb-setter. Her bag was packed; her new dress hung in the living room like a sacred banner ready to witness an oath.

I cleaned the table; Tata had another brandy.

Rinsing the cups, I asked: 'Did you call Father?'

'Good,' Tata replied distractedly, 'let him miss me.' She cocked her head to one side and eased back into the chair.

'What was in that letter?' she asked, her mind wandering. 'Any *good* news?'

'Igor needs a suit,' I said abruptly.

She turned round in her chair and fixed me with a searching stare. 'A suit? How old is he?'

She hadn't seen Igor since he was nine. He was now twelve. At eleven he was finally released from medical observation and told not to darken the clinic's door until at least the next decade. Tata had thought that Igor might want to come and live with us, which meant losing her spare bedroom – maiden pink, lace-curtained windows. She had stiffened her back and written to him – he wouldn't like it here.

She'd felt the need to gain my support and counted on our incidental similarity: we both, beyond all doubt, knew nothing about boys *that* age. Was there much to know, I thought. I wouldn't go near them – pimply brows, sweating, swearing, stealing sweets from girls, cultivating biceps, forming rough gaggles.

Take the boy next door. He used to give me rides on his bicycle – a sweet giant, I called him. Last spring he became such a nuisance his own father left the family for a totally strange woman, an overweight bricklayer. The same week this boy skipped school sports, gulped down a mug of vodka and hung himself upside down from a swing.

'White seagull, give me a kiss, wave me goodbye . . . ' he whined. Watching him from the window Tata waved her fist at him. Naturally he overreacted – plucked his *thing* out of his trousers and peed quite expertly right in our direction. Nothing there on *him* showed any signs of shrinking, I do remember that.

My father had *his* first suit when he was twenty-two. There is an out-of-focus picture of him taken by Tata. He looks spruce and lithe with a wide-brimmed hat and a vamp-style cigarette in his hand. The picture was framed and stood on Tata's bedside table; a few days before it had been replaced with a heart-shaped mirror and a book – *The Thousand and One Nights*.

Igor won't get a suit this year. She could have just said it straight – who would argue? But no, my mother wanted to make it absolute. She sat herself on the kitchen table in the spotlight: crossed legs, head thrown back. The printed cucumbers embroidering her nightgown twisted in sheer desperation.

'I got my ski boots from a dead man, never had a new pair . . . We haven't gone on holiday for three years. He just makes promises: "Oh, I'll buy you a *muffta*, take you to the hot spa . . ." He's there – I'm here. Six months apart. Then he comes home, talks gold – I water the plants. He says, "I can't share my blanket with you – I've been sleeping alone. I have to get used to you." Did I ever mind? Me? Of course not – I didn't even care, not any more . . .'

It was obvious – my mother could make do with a lizard.

While the radio played the midnight anthem she moved her bag to the front door and took her dress and the brandy to the bedroom, leaving the kitchen as if exiting a stage.

I stretched out on the chair: my feet in boy's sports shoes

100

reeked of rubber. Who cares that I don't have summer sandals and my feet are sweating . . . ? Who cares if my brother's testicles wizen to a knot . . . ?

I washed and changed, then went round the house drawing the curtains. In the living room the big window facing our kitchen garden was open. Outside, under the fluttering light of a street lamp, I saw a figure, as good as naked, untying the swing. It was in no condition to be used since one of the ropes was worn to shreds and the seat was cracked. I climbed out of the window and tripped over a tin water can which disclosed my presence.

'I want to fly . . . ' my mother said, adjusting her knee-length underpants, sagging in a crescent at the bottom. She wore nothing else. Her hair was a hayrick tousled by the wind that reddened her nose and wet her lips. She looked like a raped scarecrow.

'I'm going to fly!' She pulled at the ropes as if starting an engine.

'Of course you will,' I said, rubbing her back which bristled with goose-pimples in self-defence. 'You are flying tomorrow . . .'

She didn't.

My mother might have made another journey – the one, the doctor said, without a return ticket – but she missed this too.

That night, some time in the early hours, Tata ate half a jar of Grandma's raspberries, wiped her hands over the table-cloth (linen with dragons, made in China) and went into coma. No pulse, no breathing, consciousness free. She fainted in such an impromptu manner that her legs took away the lampstand and her head, hitting the bed table, smashed the heart-shaped mirror into bits.

Seven years' bad luck, the ambulance man proclaimed, stepping over the broken glass. He wrapped my mother in a blanket and as he was lifting her up, a bullet, buried safely in his back since the Second World War, turned anti-clock-wise. 'What did I tell you?' he said, wincing.

Tata was wheeled along the hospital corridor, where the smell of carbolic acid attempted to cover up the unwanted contents of somebody's sick stomach. My own stomach grew legs that kicked me from inside.

As the doctor on duty was leaving for a holiday resort the same morning, he dealt with Tata swiftly. She started vomiting – she was alive.

Hit on the head, the nurse emphasised, stroking Tata's kiss-curls, packed in bandages.

'Triton is gone . . . ' my mother gasped.

'You see what I mean?' The nurse glanced at me.

'She's been enlightened,' the doctor commented distantly, writing up his notes.

He asked me to follow him to the staff room, wallpapered with posters of enthusiastic microbes and mouth-to-mouth resuscitation. A nurse served us breakfast. The disinfected cutlery clanked feverishly; the tea was cold, black as the doctor's eyes, which were stained with fatigue.

'Did you know it happened to your mother once before?' He bit a lump of sugar, sipped tea. 'When she was ten . . . a bugler in a Pioneers camp. Toot-toot-too-doot! Many of us were.' She had been sent to help bring in the harvest on a collective farm, ate wild raspberries and conked out.

I imagined Tata wearing a red kerchief, a piqué panama, white garters – making history with a fanfare. I was learning about my mother's vivid past in what seemed to be the murkiest present.

What was she trying to do – poison herself? I questioned the doctor but he averted his eyes to the ceiling. They said it all.

I stood up, moved quickly to the door but tripped over the doctor's chair, spilling his tea. He snatched me back, pushed me down onto his wet knee and said, censoriously: '*My* mother once went off parachute jumping and I never saw her again.'

Oh God, I thought, sliding back onto my chair. Another one, wanting to fly.

The doctor removed his white coat, unloosened his tie.

'If there's something you might want to tell me?' he asked drowsily.

I know it now: there are some things in life which are best not talked about to a man. Padded bras, letters from aunts, a mother's earthy daydreams – dancing to a juke-box, dating a lizard. But then I talked easily as if to myself or to the microbes on the wall, who looked friendly enough to join us at the table. And when I stopped, in doubt as to where this all would lead, the doctor was asleep. A motionless lump, unshaven, smelling of tobacco and detergent. I was about to take a biscuit from his plate when he shuddered awake.

'You didn't make it all up, eh?' He caught my hand,

103

smiling most tenderly, sweet as wild raspberries . . . 'Triton the lizard!' His laughter, afflicted by a homicidal cough, brought two nurses running in.

It was a case to remember, he said, contemplating a while, chewing his words, too cautious to speak.

'A Greek protocol – did you do it at school?'

'Ye-yes . . .' I said, humouring him.

'Think mythology . . .'

I tried.

If a Triton – the doctor imparted his theory – was a godly creature, dealing with sea emotions, then my mother, one might suggest, was looking for some guidance to control the dark ocean of her own feelings. In other words, she needed to be calmed down or, maybe, stirred up like a storm. He frowned, sighing, and added: '*Women* – they never know what they want . . .' his shorthand message for *your mother should have her head examined.*

'My mother wanted a French beret,' I confessed, fidgeting.

'It doesn't matter, it's all Greek . . . ' The doctor drummed on the table, his fingers stained with iodine. 'She's missing your father. A sorry business.' He breathed out, shrugged. I blinked agreeably, getting into the spirit.

The ambulance arrived to pick up the doctor. That Saturday morning he was flying to a seaside resort in the Crimea, with his wife (to whom he'd been married 'all his life'), their suitcases and a fishing rod for two.

Fishing, he said, saved his marriage. His own remedy – prescribed to nobody else as yet.

I went home, cleaned up Tata's bedroom and tried to fix the

lampstand which was beyond repair. I replaced *The Thousand and One Nights* with my father's picture, and on the way back to hospital called in at the radio hut.

Kit tuned in to me briskly, a thundering solo: Where's your mother? Why didn't she call? What's she up to?

'She's breaking the furniture,' I said.

'Bad line. Repeat!' Kit's voice pierced through the static.

The radio operator fiddled fiercely with the knobs.

'Get back home!' he barked into the ether, dabbing my eyes with the hem of his shirt.

SEVEN

···

IT STARTED SNOWING heavily the night Kit bought Tata new
ski boots; her old ones – from a dead man – were bestowed
upon me. Trying them on stalled my words of gratitude: the
boots were in immaculate condition, weighed a ton, and
laced up tight as shackles. Nobody seemed to remember
that I'd never skied or had my own pair of skis before.

The snowstorm haunted my parents. They stayed up late
holding hands, watching the flakes falling down the win-
dow-pane. I didn't see much of them in those days, which
were agreed as their repair break before our summer
holidays. We planned to go camping on the Black Sea coast,
sail off some wild beaches, get tar-tanned and pot-bellied
with fruit. Grapes and pineapples were the most desirable
items in our imaginary menu.

We slept late, for my lessons began after lunch and lasted
until six. The stove was kept running all day, although from
the next week it would no longer be my father's responsibility: he had hired a stoker. Just for the time being, he said,
while he was busy resting. My mother gave him a meaning-
ful glance.

Day and night they confined themselves to the bedroom.
At breakfast Tata would appear highly inflamed – her face
and neck crusty red, as if rubbed with a loofah. I was

concerned: she'd been taken seriously ill not so long ago ('food poisoning' we called it).

Kit agreed with me that some fresh air would do no harm to either of them, but Tata said she wasn't after 'ventilating herself' or dressing up. In fact, her negligée showed more than it covered. She puckered her eyes looking at Kit, his loosened pyjamas bottoms and his bare chest, which he paraded like a peacock would its tail. He didn't shriek though.

The stoker came in the morning, covert as a thief. I heard steps rustling through the hall; the kitchen door gave out a squeak, then closed. The house was warming up; the winter light turned pale blue, braiding the curtains.

I had a good enough excuse for going to the kitchen – I was hungry. Near the stove, throbbing with heat, was a pile of neatly arranged clothes, each item furrier than the next: a soldier's sheepskin coat, an astrakhan hat, a deerskin boot. Wet from fresh washing, the floorboards shone glossily; I walked straight in and slipped.

'Oh, shshsh . . . ' the cupboard door shushed at me. It was half open, slamming two small feet trapped inside. Too big for a mouse, I thought. The head poked out, dark-eyed, dark-haired, ears sticking up; one earring curved the same way as the nose, pecking a moustache.

'Where do you keep flour?'

'In the pantry if we have any . . .'

'Get it.'

I brought the flour. Dangling off the chair the little feet

tapped a soundless rhythm, the head rose above the table on a level with the teapot, the body was invisible.

'The Sabre Dance is my favourite tune . . . what's yours?' the head asked, the earring jiggling.

It must be a *she*, a she-stoker, I thought, gazing, and no longer than a sabre herself.

'I like old songs . . . "The Peasant and the Frost",' I said, and pulled the stool out from under the table.

'Oh no, don't sit *there*.' The stoker punched the flour bag which burst into a dusty cloud. 'Not with your back to the door.'

This advice left me puzzled.

'Always face those who might come in without invitation,' she clarified her point and added more pronouncedly: 'The good old motto of the inmates.'

It was evident that our stoker was one of them. Mixing the flour, she rolled up the sleeves of her shirt, disclosing the inky blots of a tattoo on her arm. I moved my stool to the furthest corner.

'You've been in prison?'

'I've been everywhere.' She slid off the chair and climbed back to sit on her knees within reach of her workplace. Changing position made her more comfortable for the issuing of orders: 'Let's dance together, I won't eat you . . .'

She wanted meat dumplings for *breakfast*.

'Why not? I never know when I'll eat again.'

She rolled the dough, cut it into circles which we stuffed with meat as minced up as her story.

A child of Armenian convicts, she was born on the great Siberian River Lena ('in prison'), grew up running away from orphanages, served her first sentence at seventeen ('paid my parents a visit') . . . was married to a huntsman, drove a lorry, was convicted again ('got to be a habit'). Released during the war, she settled in Magadan, but had recently moved up to Seimchan – 'close to nature and a private bath unit'.

Currently she was working as a stoker at the settlement heating station, living there in the extension of the staff washroom. Her bed was a bath bench, her table a log of firewood; everything else, including her clothes, was given in exchange for a free wash, under the counter.

'Come one day,' she said. 'You'll have the steam room all to yourself.'

Tonight, I agreed expeditiously, not waiting to be asked twice. Every washing at our public bathhouse compounded my misery at being gawkily framed; there would always be someone (or my mother herself) commenting on my lack of substance with the gravitas of a newsreader.

Tonight? The stoker reconsidered, the expression in her eyes changing, as if she was wondering about keeping to the offer.

Her dumplings, identical and perfectly shaped – about a hundred dough hearts – filled the tray in a grand heart-like formation. My plate was spread with sticky, undernourished meat-pods which split while being cooked. Just the thing for the stoker who liked mushy food because several of her teeth had forgotten to grow. Growing had never been her strong point. Her height had stayed unchanged since she was ten.

I ate away at her hearts till my stomach bulged, rumbling

at the strain, but the plate in front of me was laden again. Finally I felt I was a single great dumpling, hot and fat, ready to be forked.

The stove was refuelled; the kettle had just whistled its second summons for my parents to get up and have their breakfast when the stoker consulted her watch distractedly. She hopped off her chair onto her furry vestments.

'You do remind me of one of my old friends,' she said, disappearing into her sheepskin coat. 'Kon-cor-dia . . . she was a circus gymnast, all skin and bones, limbs jumping . . . Didn't last long. She would skip over the camp fence and back again – just teasing the guards. They shot at her and shouted: "*Allez, Koka, allez . . .*" '

At the front door we shook hands (manly, you could say). The stoker proclaimed with an air of finality that she would call me Koka, *just* Koka.

'What's your name?'

'You don't know!' She pretended that my ignorance offended her. I played her game, humbled my head, halved my smile.

'Call me Ararat. Just Ararat . . .'

The woman shared her name with a mountain that was supposedly the resting place of Noah's Ark.

'She tells lies – in *mountains*,' Tata warned me.

Kit added: 'She drinks spirits.'

'Gallons!' Tata rounded her eyes.

We were having dinner in the living room, by candlelight. The settlement was drowned in darkness as our power station, used to irregular supplies, was saving on fuel. Twice

110

this week the head teacher had to shorten the timetable, cancelling lessons, an announcement that incited an Olympic hurrah in every classroom.

Today, in my excitement, I had picked up somebody else's hat, for which its owner promptly pushed me through the front door, headfirst. I rolled down the porch steps, sliding a lengthy distance across the courtyard, and lost my gloves and keys in the snow.

When Tata let me in I felt my head had been stuck with ice needles.

'If you get meningitis, don't come home,' she said, slipping into the living room. There the table was laid: candles flickered, champagne frothed in funnel-shaped glasses.

'*Love token, half-broken, no logic, no luck . . .*' Kit played the piano, singing some poisoned romance off-key. I wasn't expected.

Getting out of my coat I knelt on an iron trivet close to the stove. Barely lit, the kitchen looked smaller, somewhat distorted, with shady corners, the ceiling a rippling sphere. Hidden below the table the stack of firewood replaced the stools that were set together along the wall, forming a bench. They were topped with rumpled paper and brushwood – the stoker must have already prepared the fuel for the morning's heating. So I'd missed her 'late' shift this evening.

'She left half an hour ago,' said Kit, 'and good for you that she did.'

The woman had been drunk and chopped the wood on the kitchen doorstep, letting chips and *chippy* words spray around. I watched Kit lighting a cigarette with practised polish; his outsized grin indicated that he wouldn't mind making use of some of her sharp *unbecoming* expressions.

'The stoker asked about you.' Tata entered the kitchen with a glass in her hand. 'She thinks you've been fed on camp rations.'

Kit laughed; the logs under the table shook queasily and toppled down. One spiky lump rolled over my foot – which was still frozen, lacking feeling, but I whined sufficiently to prove I was hurt. Heading towards me, Tata tripped and knocked the rubbish bucket over, thus compounding the wreckage.

'Oh hell, devil's well . . . ' Tata said in a huff. 'Have some champagne.' She handed me her glass: a few bubbles in the bottom, a lipstick print on the side. I nursed it into the living room.

Another bottle, cold and frosty, was opened. The cork hit the ceiling and ricocheted off the piano keys.

'C-sharp,' Kit echoed authoritatively, filling their glasses and a mug for me.

I seasoned the froth with sugar and drank it sensibly between portions of corned beef and vermicelli, made from Ararat's dough. Some of her heart dumplings enriched our main course, disappearing fast. Tata pinched the last heart, snuggling it on her plate, and fed it to Kit. He almost ate her fingers, too, smacking and licking his lips. For such manners I would be sent off to the pigsty – but my mother presided over the table admiring him. Wet-mouthed, Kit roared and sank his teeth into her elbow which sustained this attack impassively.

Once, when I'd lullabyed a toddler, a free-living Hercules,

112

he had sucked in the whole of my thumb. I didn't like it. That was a love game, Tata had said and washed my hand in antiseptic.

Having a retentive memory, my thumb tended to bear a grudge long after the accident and did so now. I dunked it in a butter dish and oiled the remembered sting by stirring the melting clots to a mush. This brought my parents to their senses.

'Manners!' said Tata.

'Are you still hungry?' asked Kit. 'Have some more vermicelli – it filled me up better than meat.' He reached for the saucepan.

'This will go to the dogs . . .' Tata pulled the saucepan to her. 'It's just dough, not vermicelli.'

I felt somehow that our stoker's culinary efforts were being deliberately belittled. 'Ararat is a good cook,' I said.

'What's that?' Tata lowered her eyes as though she'd received a kick under the table. 'What did we call her?'

'Ararat.'

'Nobody calls her *that* – she's Raya.'

'She was named after a mountain,' I said firmly.

'She tells lies – in *mountains*,' Tata warned me.

'She can dance with sabres,' I protested moderately, but it just sounded as if I was trying to persuade myself.

'Exactly what I've just said.' Tata smiled a winning smile.

Between the hiccups that came with his share of champagne Kit added: 'She drinks spirits.'

'Gallons!' Tata prompted him jarringly and poured the rest of the champagne into her glass. She drained it with a controlled fury and resumed: 'And lives by her wits; no shame.'

I sat feeling ill at ease, contemplating the empty mug. Kit affected not to say a word, for his hand was finding its way to Tata's knee. When it got there, she jolted embarrassedly and with a single sigh put the two candles out. Smelling of waxy smoke, the darkness resounded with jeering whispers: typical *avanturistka* . . .

Typical, Kit parroted, with smacking sounds.

Wears her tattoos like pearls . . .

Pearls . . . (aggravated smacking).

I slid off my chair and made a move to the door. 'What's *avanturistka*?' I asked.

Kit chuckled, breathing like a chain pump.

'Don't we say something before leaving the table?' Tata said in a husky voice.

I went to the kitchen and took out of the cupboard an old Russian glossary that was supporting a broken shelf. '. . . Derived from the French – the same as adventuress,' it said, 'a confidence trickster . . .'

Nice word, I thought. Never mind the French.

I read *The Three Musketeers* before going to sleep. At nine o'clock the settlement's electricity returned for an hour allowing domestic chores to be done. I'd read the book three times (twice back to front) and memorised the best of the epic to the last detail: the descriptions of seventeenth-century boudoirs, period courtesies and dress etiquette, jewels pro rata, verbal and duelling dramas – all of which failed to blend well with my teacher's objectives.

114

If you prefer Dumas to *our* classics, I was told at school, get a taste of French history out of him, not just the adventures.

At the end of term I wrote a compulsory essay to mark my literary sensibility and inner ripening. To be on the safe side I tasted the courtly life and times of Louis XIII using a serving spoon – the vast introduction to the book compiled by a Frenchified lady critic.

We both did satisfactorily, considering my teacher's wary report. She was unaware of this ingenious co-authorship, since in her own words she had learned most of her French history from *War and Peace*. On the other hand she felt strongly about my 'irrational' attitude towards the main characters. My favourite was Aramis, gentle as his name, which sounded like a flower to me.

'But he's only a *third* musketeer!' exclaimed Albina Petrovna, my teacher, admitting her fondness, naturally, for d'Artagnan, 'a positive hero, number one'.

She idolised Constansia, a maid-of-honour, a darling dove although a shady brunette. I was fascinated by her competitor Miladi, a natural blonde, in spite of her being 'a negative character of the first grade'. So what? She was utterly French, I thought, almost perfect (if it wasn't for her shoulder, branded with a tattoo), a pampered *petite* who loved living dangerously.

'Think again.' My teacher insisted on getting a clear definition of my heart's bearings. I remember sitting somewhat blank-faced, drawing arrows across my exercise book.

'Who do you think you fancy?' Albina Petrovna nearly expired in anticipation. 'A beheaded courtesan?'

She shouldn't have mentioned *that* – it made me sick at heart just to turn over the slaughter page. So much for French gallantry: to correct a perfectly genteel woman by chopping her little head off, her curls like bells.

'That's better, get it out of your system,' said Albina Petrovna as my arrows grew wet and smudged. She shared her blotting paper with me.

The Three Musketeers got flattened under my pillow as I slept wrapped up in Grandma's 'peasant' shawl, patching its moth-eaten holes with my dreams.

There was a different ending to the story which, that night, I saw in a new perspective – dramatically simple: Miladi didn't die, she was allowed to keep her little head right there on her branded shoulders. She was arrested and sent to the Bastille, where everybody expected her to be remoulded into a fine, regular being. A shepherdess or a seamstress. Instead she ran away with a guard. Since her gross livelihood had gone with the wind she wore her rose tattoo like a pearl – a true adventuress to the bone . . .

The next morning I was up at six o'clock. First things first – to heat the stove; it took me some time to negotiate the smoke and start the wood burning.

I brushed the floor, washed the dishes left soaking in the tub since last night, made tea and buckwheat porridge, fried the 'Kievskaya' sausage – the thickest lumps spitting fat. The kitchen was tropically hot with the door closed and window sealed, reflecting in a dim mirror of morning twilight a table laid for two. But there was no sign of my guest arriving. Our stoker was inexcusably late.

I thought of surprising Ararat, doing her job in exchange for company and perhaps another hearty talk, a joke to spare. I would tell her *my* story, show her our scrapbook of photos and the collection of my milk-teeth kept in an old hammered-out tin which was quite a thing itself. Found in the attic, the tin, clanging like a rattle, contained a clod of fishing hooks and one rusty ring, a forged piece of history that should fit Ararat's ear perfectly. Or a fishing hook as a ready-to-wear earring – I could adjust it for her in no time.

The clock's hand passed eight; the kettle boiled, grumbling. I heard our neighbour shut himself in an outdoor lavatory, whistle a dawn overture and shoot back home.

Right! I went into the hall, pulled my felt boots on, starchy from the famishing cold. What's the saying? If the mountain won't come to Mahomet, he goes to the mountain.

The yard, covered in snow that had been falling all morning, was streaked with a tangled map of footsteps. The neighbour was emptying the pail when I greeted him outside the gate.

'Early . . . ' he said and peered at me as though I had walked naked into the snowdrift. He was still in his pyjamas, identical to Kit's, only rather worn, and wet around the fly.

Avoiding making further discoveries I turned away from him and paused before jumping over the rubbish heap to the rammed-down path connected to the main road.

Sheathed in silence the settlement was slowly rising. The windows gazed out, lit up, some half-curtained; porches were unswept but doors jingled open, letting out steam, clouds of exhilarating mist. The smoke, drifting from the

117

chimneys, sparkled with fire mites, almost instantly snuffed out by swirls of flakes that padded the sky, muffled the trees.

Near the park entrance the militia jeep passed me by, chafing its wheels, howling its siren. The same to you, I thought, and blew my nose which needed more than this brief attention, for it didn't know whether to lead me on or stop.

I was supposed to be halfway to the heating station where Ararat worked and lived, but being rather heated myself, I was circling around the park getting nowhere. Maybe I was bothering too much about nothing. Who was *I* to expect this woman to be at my feet every morning? Who was *she* making me rush to her like Mahomet's twin?

Talking it over I did another circuit, then crossed the park and came up with more questions than answers. By that time my nose had stiffened to a carrot, turning its frostbitten end in one firm direction: home.

The gate to our courtyard stood open, swinging across the path ploughed by sledge runners. I followed the tracks and stumbled into the back end of the barn, where the washing-line hung in discreet retreat. The bed sheets, frost-eaten, swished with a crusty sound and came apart, giving way for our stoker's head.

'Where have you been?' she had the nerve to ask me.

'You were late!' I screeched.

'No.' She pushed herself through the bed sheets and stood in front of me on her toes, prancing. 'I wasn't late – I came on time, saw you were busy with the stove and went off shopping . . .'

'When did you come? What shopping?' I shouted stiffly. 'The shops don't open till nine!'

'Who said *shopping*?' She gave a quick look around – all saintly innocence: 'I was *busy* too.'

I couldn't refrain from snorting, but Aarat, not the least unnerved, volunteered the news: she wouldn't be working for us any longer. 'I've just quit.'

She bent her lips in a timid smile and added hastily: 'Your mother let me down.'

She'd had a clash with Tata over the dough.

'I left it yesterday *rising* in a mixing bowl and she wasted it on vermicelli . . . How could she!' In asking, Ararat squinted her eyes towards the end of the washing-line where Tata's bras and winter panties were flapping. 'It was my dough, *my* lazy pancakes!' That's what she had apparently said confronting my mother, still in bed, half an hour ago.

'Nothing here is *yours*,' my mother had declared quite matter-of-factly and promptly showed Ararat to the door.

I'd never tried lazy pancakes (nor indeed heard of them) but reflected on their loss with a mournful grin.

'I knew you would understand,' Ararat muttered, sadness inhabiting her face. The constant change of her temper began to strain me. Presently the bashful smile was rearranging her pained expression.

'Could you do me a favour?' she whined, plucking at my scarf. It sounded like Ararat was trading off for the wasted dough.

She asked me to take a little sack (a parcel rather) to her

119

friend's house, insisting on strict confidence: nobody should know where it was going or who had sent it. 'A night-time delivery – the later the better.'

'What's in there?' I asked, probably overvigilant.

'It's personal,' she said, 'but *breakable*. Needs to be handled with care.'

She went on delivering the lengthy list of instructions which I was told to repeat at speed. When Ararat considered I was ready to fit the bill, she kissed me three times, then with equal intensity wiped her snow-dusted sleeve over my running nose. Despite being slightly disconcerted by this final touch, I realised that the sack, the parcel or whatever it was, hadn't been granted to me yet.

'It's in your bedroom – the *cat* is under the bed!' Ararat hissed, her feet tapping excitedly. She tightened her belt round her coat and bounded off, a little furry cracker.

You call it a parcel, I thought, struggling to lift it. More like a camel-load, a solid dead-weight. It was packed into my father's rucksack (his loyal attendant in the field, striped green and advancing in years). How 'stripey' – as the rucksack was known –· got into Ararat's hands I couldn't say, but she certainly didn't shy away from things that belonged to somebody else.

There was yet more evidence of this: my sledge, with its rope broken since last winter, had been dragged out of the barn's dankest corner, mended and had its runners polished with grease.

'Take a sledge, it's handy.' My mind recalled Ararat's instructions. But she hadn't said what I was to do with 'stripey' while I was at school. I couldn't leave it on its own till nightfall. Tata was inclined to get restless, poking her nose everywhere once Kit got tired of giving her the time of day.

As soon he went skiing that morning, Tata put her apron on and armed herself with a broom. A spring cleaning at the end of October! I hoped she was recovered enough to return to work.

I lugged 'stripey' out under the discordance of the vacuum cleaner and radio news blasting in the background. This was a sufficient cover for me to cross the yard unnoticed and after fastening 'stripey' to the sledge I set off for the road.

The first lessons at school had already started; the corridor expanded with the silence preceding registration.

I was pleased to miss maths, as I didn't hate our teacher *that* much to face him with 'stripey' in my arms and no homework to show. There were two lessons ahead – English and biology – neither my favourite.

The biology teacher, a middle-aged woman, who wore hats at school and wigs in public (somebody said she was shaving her head to initiate hair growth), called us 'maggots', but promised that all of us, without exception, would eventually grow into something beautiful: a 'beetle or a butterfly'.

Our English teacher was a fine lady on her own, truly a butterfly, quite hairy though, as some butterflies are. Tina Salomonovna spoke French, which she'd learned at the Moscow Pedagogical Institute, and English picked up in India where her husband, a civil engineer, was constructing a dam. Salomon (we abbreviated her name) also made herself understood in some Hindu dialect that sounded very much like her English – and vice versa. However, she claimed to speak all her languages like a native and her English conformed to the rule – for everyone in India has apparently grown up bilingual. One couldn't help it, we were told, considering the country's colonial past.

My English past was a history of bad marks and inconsistent attendance. I liked English but Salomon didn't like me, partly because I had trouble grasping any of her jokes in whatever language she chose to speak. I even failed to smile – that counted as another petty point against me. Smiling is to the English, she said once, what soul is to Russians. If only I'd known the latter to start with.

She came to the class before the bell rang; the maths teacher was still writing on the blackboard. I pulled 'stripey' nearer the door, waiting to slip in.

'Moving house?' Salomon asked in Russian and then commented in English with a saturnine smile: 'The house that Jack built?'

We wrote down a dictation, 'What I have, had, will have or never will', a snowball of grammar growing bigger with every lesson, when Salomon remembered to take revenge on me. She moved closer to my desk (where 'stripey' lay half-tucked under my feet) and stood unequivocally in Napoleon's assertive stance.

'*What does she have there?*' she asked the class, not without a touch of disdain which we'd all got used to.

'She has a *beeeg* bag,' said Vova, our class upstart, a four-eyed wunderkind who sat in the row next to me.

'Zis is *not* her beeeg bag,' corrected Vova's friend, a right sponger and a dandruff victim.

'What does she have in her *big* bag?' Salomon ignored him, stressing the correct pronunciation.

'A pen and a rubber,' dandruff struck again, pleased with himself.

Salomon looked down at 'stripey' and up at me, urging the answer that would spare her further efforts.

'I don't know,' I said, embracing 'stripey' with my feet.

It was as though a chill had captured Salomon's body.

'Can't you be more articulate for once?' she said and shuddered, her face suggesting some inexpressible ordeal.

I would have escaped right after English – preferably home and without 'stripey', shaking off those looks I had acquired in excess during the lesson. But the break caught me queuing in the lavatory. So I missed my chance to get away before the biology teacher arrived for class. She shut the door in my face just as I'd made my mind up to enter.

Hiding away in an uninhabited corner, the attic staircase, I overheard a conversation from down below.

Our school cook was talking to her husband, the militia-man Lukov, who had come to collect the kitchen leftovers for his Alsatian and her newborn puppies. He told Tonya the news: there had been a break-in at the food warehouse this morning.

'What was stolen?' Tonya cried.

'Rations,' said Lukov and sighed solemnly. 'Vodka, monkey-nuts, cracknels . . .'

'Oh, *mamochka*!' Tonya whined, clapped her hands. 'Who did it?'

'Uncle Vanya . . . ,' Lukov growled at her. 'How do *I* know . . . the old bitch messed up the scent again . . .'

'Oh, be fair,' Tonya drawled in distress. 'She just gave birth . . .'

'I'm not talking about the dog,' Lukov said reproachfully. His heels clicked impatiently.

He mentioned the name of the warehouse keeper, a working war veteran suspected of staging burglaries. Somebody said she still practised her partisan methods and feared no one. So when a monthly 'misreckoning' happened – crates of vodka, tins of preserves or chocolates gone missing – this was all written off as 'transportation losses' and no more action was taken.

The militiaman scraped his feet: 'I'm not fit to do this job,' he bleated. 'My corns . . . killing me . . .'

'Have *kotletka*, Papa,' his wife urged, letting him into the kitchen.

The bell rang at six; the last lesson, floor exercises, started in the gymnasium. Five minutes later I scooted out of the building, meeting nobody. I thought: at least some luck's running my way.

Before I'd set foot on the road I was offered a lift. Well, it was no use agonising over it for I had a long journey ahead and an endless one back.

And there we were, cramped but cheerful, wheeling towards number 32 Forest Street.

'I thought you were off home,' said Lukov, driving his jeep through the slush. 'Forest Street . . . it's out of my way,' he moaned, but I didn't budge.

'Visiting someone?' He'd submitted, if rather unwillingly.

'Just a friend,' I said, cuddling 'stripey' on my knees.

I was sitting on the front seat that usually would be occupied by Lukov's Alsatian, who wasn't sure whether to give it up or camp on my shoulders. Finally she forced herself in between me and her owner.

'Good girl, Bukva,' Lukov crowed softly and a comforting, velvety tongue slithered across his face.

The cabin was perspiring, the windows streaming as if rain was seeping through. Bukva kept sneezing, banging her head against 'stripey', which clanked sourly in return.

'What's in there?' Lukov asked with a friendly wink.

'A pen and a rubber,' I said.

He made a clucking noise and asked no more, having a sneezing fit himself. It's not catching, he told me when I ducked my nose into my scarf – more like an 'occupational hazard' I gathered from Lukov's unintelligible complaint. Both he and his Bukva had been exposed at the warehouse to a man-made poison applied to divert noses from all trace of the burglary.

'Whoever it was covered up their scent with tobacco . . .' he mused, and chuckled as though taking a pinch of snuff. '*Kazbek Authentic* . . . I used to smoke but I don't recommend it – very strong stuff, throw any scent haywire.'

'What are you going to do?' I asked absently, feeling sweat trickling down my legs.

'Go fishing! Your father promised to show me some places. The salmon there – woooo . . .'

He spread his arms wide, letting the jeep zigzag across the road. Another driver, heading towards us, screeched to a

125

halt. With admonishing gestures Lukov hooted at him three times ('Idiot you are!') and, with his eyes alert for once, drew close to me.

'It's funny, you know,' he confided, bemused. 'I thought I couldn't smell *anything* . . . but,' he sniffed at me, 'you smell of vodka.' He rubbed his nose. 'Have you been drinking?'

Very funny, I pouted. Sorry, Lukov said, withdrawing his accusation, explaining that lately he'd become paranoid, suspecting everyone of wrong-doings everywhere. Of course, I said, I understood, and nodded, paying tribute to his vigilance. He cursed the steering wheel, and sneezed out: 'Vodka is a killer.' So was his breath, it robbed me of my senses.

My recovery, slow-fused, nerves tingling, followed after Lukov discharged me a few houses away from number 32. Tramping through the snow, I stood wondering why I was wet from the waist down. My best school stockings were sodden, saturated with something sharp and peppery.

I was still holding 'stripey', heavier than ever, and when I rolled him onto the sledge he turned turtle and flashed his soggy bottom at me. In fact, he was leaking through several bullet-like holes. Not you, old sack, I prayed – don't do this to me. Where do I go from here?

Straight – along the hardened snow path, round the slide, the washing-line, back to the path, left, right, wrong door, a dog-pen, a dog's mess – and no number 32, not a sign. Number 31 was a barn, without windows, secured with a pan-shaped padlock. Next door had set up a mini-fence, just above my knee, imaginatively built to separate two trees that moved their spooky, crooked twigs towards me. As I approached them, they hooked together nervously, trembling, and when I looked again I saw two reindeer baring their teeth at me.

'Kss . . . kss . . .' I said, and they let me pass by in one piece. Deer don't eat *us*, we eat *them* – I reasoned, sobering myself up by dragging the sledge as fast I could until, as if hitting the brakes, it skidded and stood on end.

'Where do you think you are going?' I was asked by someone who pulled the rope out of my hands.

'Deer *here*, deer *there*,' I thought I shouted, but didn't hear a word. The ghostly horns were gouging out my ribs. It took me some time to clear my vision and recognise, somewhere down below, Ararat, on tiptoe, dressed in fur overalls and a top ornamented with beads and tassels, in Chukchi style.

'Are you all right, Koka?' She pinched me on the cheek, or was that a kiss done her way? She whistled, then froze; an owl-like crying, growing froggy, echoed back.

'Say *Eetti*,' Ararat ordered me, at attention, brushing my fringe out of my eyes.

'*Eetti*.'

'Not *now*. Say it to my friend.'

She towed the sledge, spoke loud, soft, humorously, full of apologies. She had mistakenly given me the wrong address, her friend had got lost; she had had to find him first, then look for me.

We walked to a pile of logs, high as a wall, a smoking wall behind which a Chukchi man was tending a campfire. He sat on a *narta* (a Chukchi sledge) and blew into the heaped scraps of paper and twigs.

'*Eetti*,' I said experimentally.

127

He glanced at me and nodded. Ararat introduced us: Teulin was his name, Koka was mine.

'Sit!' She pushed me down on the front of my sledge and emptied 'stripey' at the other end.

'It's leaking,' I advised. My legs went bandy, wet and itchy under the knees.

'It *was*.' Ararat regarded me coldly, ripping open a bundle of newspaper, squashed and drippy. She produced a handful of broken glass – a litre of peppered vodka reduced to teardrops.

The rest of it had done a good job on 'stripey' and me (one point to Lukov), my stockings to be precise. The candies, *Little Bear in the North*, were crushed into a soggy mess, though a pack of honey wafers and a sack of monkey-nuts ('Yours, Koka,' said Ararat with glum satisfaction) had survived.

'And that's for you.' She'd turned to Teulin, whose sooty eyes were gazing anxiously at 'stripey': two bottles of vodka (intact), a tin of fruit-drops and a packet of poppy cracknels. He shoved his fur hood back and his face split into a smile. His front teeth were missing, his hair twisted in two plaits, tied with ribbon.

'Is he a *he*?' I asked Ararat, while Teulin poured some vodka on a poppy cracknel and sucked it like a thumb.

'Very much so,' she said, admiring his gastronomic chivalry.

Husband to a number of wives, he was Ararat's 'old trouble' whom she met occasionally when he got out of his wives' clutches.

If I wished Teulin well, Ararat advised me, better not tell

128

anyone that we met or that I had fetched him vodka. I didn't like the way she put it.

'I *fetched* him nothing – you did.'

'But you brought it here, in your father's bag!' Ararat burst into laughter with complacent triumph.

'*You* gave me the bag!'

'Me?' she sneered. 'The cat was under your bed.' She resumed her laughter, a parody of a trumpet, filling me with permanent, clinical hysteria.

I sat for a while, unloosing my thoughts and the scarf that rubbed my neck like a tightened lasso. She frowned, watching me.

'*Vanlyarkin?*' Teulin soaked another cracknel in vodka and held it out to me.

'That's a lazy pancake for you,' Ararat said in a careful, harsh voice. 'Not as good as mine, but . . .' She tautened her lips. 'Do you want one, Koka?'

I chose a blob of snow instead and washed my hands. They felt piping hot, oil thrown on a fire.

'I'll take you home,' Ararat said, glancing quickly at Teulin. He cleared his throat, becoming animated; it looked like he sensed that she was about to leave him. Ararat talked to him in a dissatisfied manner, as if to a child who needed to be put straight.

'*Inne* . . . *Itke* . . .' he moaned, and drew in his breath.

Ararat checked her pockets and came out with a little sack, an old napkin wrapped into a pouch, which she tossed to and fro like a hand grenade before throwing it across to Teulin.

'Eeeee . . .' Teulin chuckled. He stuffed his pipe with tobacco from the pouch. 'Kazbek, *velinkikun* . . .' he cried with an affection that visibly touched Ararat.

'Kazbek . . . you bet!' she coughed out.

'It's poison,' I said, sagging inside my coat.

'One man's poison, another man's pleasure . . .' She contradicted me with a round of shaking and gripping of my hands.

'It poisoned Bukva . . . and Lukov,' I said and repeated it louder as if being called to testify against the vocational handicaps of warehouse burglary. Ararat seemed to understand what I was saying, a fact which she recognised by admitting in a hostile tone, 'The dog shouldn't have been there. She's on maternity leave.'

Ararat would never have harmed old Bukva, of course, though she'd happily duped me.

She'd meant no wrong: Teulin was coming. She'd promised to treat him to lazy pancakes and vodka. And what did she have at the end of the day? She twisted her fingers in a combination that figuratively speaking meant 'a thing of naught'.

When she had passed the warehouse this morning, the door was wide open, well, it was not *properly* locked (she corrected herself) – and nobody was there, not a soul. She'd taken nothing: clenched her fists and walked away, although not without misgivings. But being indecisive was never her favourite state of mind. Approaching our house she'd found a nerve in her system that directed her to take advantage of the situation. Moreover, she'd had a vision of me, hunger-stricken or feast-driven (or both), which gathered momentum and turned into action.

As I was in the kitchen making our breakfast, she had rummaged through the barn and come out with her first two collaborators: my sledge and my father's rucksack.

There were *tons* of things in the warehouse she would have liked to have laid her hands on – and her teeth. 'If you have any . . .' I snapped, rather obtrusively helping her to loosen the confessional thread.

'Oh poor Bukva, her dribbling tits . . .' she cried in an exasperated pitch.

Exhausted by the mental effort of making any sense out of this troubled conversation, Teulin stood beside her in a cloud of smoke.

She had to be careful to leave no trace. 'Wouldn't you?' Ararat asked, alternating her desperate gaze between Teulin and me. 'To be *locked up* for a pack of candies and a sorry tipple?'

'Lukov said . . .' I started, seizing her arm.

'Lukov is a castrated baboon!' Ararat cried. She would like to lock him in the warehouse and pickle him in vodka and spirit vinegar. There were r-i-i-ivers of it there, and brandy. 'Five star' batteries of crates – while the shops were empty, swept clean. Well, of course, what's new?

'You called me Koka and set me up.' I stooped to the level of her eyes.

'Yes.' She brushed my fringe back. 'I did – and you got away with it . . .'

EIGHT

TATA CONVINCED herself that I had had *it* ('thought you never would') – my first night out, for better or worse, which obviously could have gone better. For she saw me coming back home: 'So late, so droopy and fooling no one – wrapped in tears . . .'

She asked me where I'd been. I said: 'Out.'

This furnished her with something to chew on till morning. By then I'd developed a rending cough that harassed our neighbours who knocked on my bedroom wall and started to play the phonograph: '*Oh, Frost, Brother Frost, don't finish me off and my trusty horse. Oh, Frost, oh-oh, ho-ho, ho-ha!*'

I pulled the blanket over my head, cutting the song off, shifting the scenery.

Lukov squeezes in, crawling on top of me, falling full weight.

'Here she is!' he blares, shaking my shoulders, twisting my head.

I crack and spew, spurting it out. Lukov is drenched, his face a slimy slug.

'Forty-degree proof!' he booms. 'Bottle her up, finish her off . . . Oh-ho, ho-ho, ho-ha!'

I howl and croak, a hollow carafe inside.

Easyeasyeasy.

My mother's minty voice, like a murmur of reminiscence, fanned down on me, tingling, cooling:

You had a temperature, a bad one, almost forty.

Your cough is better now, yes, much nicer. *Do* mind my face, that's it . . .

This blanket again . . . don't you start, I'm telling you – let it go!

So I did. I kept sheltering under the blanket but Tata would fetch me out. She shook me and twisted me, turning me from back to sides while running a cloth over my body. I seemed to be dissolving in sweat. Then her voice shrilled coldly: into the *bucket*, please, be a good girl.

Well, I didn't; dizzy as a spindle I hung down and threw up somewhere behind the bucket, onto her knees.

If it makes you feel better, Tata said, with grim contempt.

'Cuckoo.'

Sitting beside my bed, Kit gave me that honeyed look, and a cup of hot water with honey stirred in.

'Lukov asked about you,' he said, grinning. 'He must be telepathic.'

'Why?' I drew the blanket up to my chin.

'Why?' Kit stared, leaning over me – an overpowering gaze. 'You cursed Lukov blue all day long!'

'Of course it must be a nightmare,' he reasoned, relaxing his eyebrows, 'to see a militiaman in your dreams . . .'

Go, I tried to hypnotise him, not bothering to speak – you are raising my temperature.

'We have a stomach cold that got chesty.' Tata sent a

message to school, protecting us from any potential visitors, and thus kept me under strict quarantine for most of the week. Kit returned to work, but my mother was determined to stay at home and look after me as if I were her last living relative, departing too soon.

I became tired of her constant, obsessive pestering and pretended to be asleep whenever I heard her coming into the bedroom.

'Sweaty,' she would call after an hour or so, 'let's do some sticking . . .'

The mustard plasters, slapped on my chest and back, set my skin burning. It might hurt a little, she said, as the mustard was freshly brewed. Another minute and I saw myself wreathed in flames, setting fire to the house.

I whispered and shouted, delirious words which Tata classified as something close to 'obscene poetry'. To silence me she recited conjugations of German irregular verbs, or read aloud: country rhymes, weather bulletins, *Masha and the Three Bears*.

Once she picked up *The Three Musketeers* and opened it at the page where the bookmark was.

'. . . none of that really mattered: Cardinal Richelieu liked to travel incognito.' She started to thumb over the lines, reading with the intonation of a vagabond story-teller. My grasp of reality suddenly returned, the burning ceased, the flames died down.

'None of that!' I shouted, my bellicose anger directed at my mother, who dropped the book on the floor. 'Read to yourself!'

I plunged under the blanket and banged my head on the

wall. This sharpened my sensory perceptions to a point: never again would I lose myself in an 'adventure' – of any kind or nature. Yes, I was past caring for these freebooters, threesomes or solo, the restless souls. I'd got to know one of them, that pocket mountain with an avalanche of trouble.

My mother had told me; she'd spelled out her full table of warnings about bad influences for which I'd given her no credit.

'I'll *always*, *always* listen to you.' I kissed my mother's knee through her thick worsted stockings.

She looked at me with impassive curiosity, disorientated rather, then blamed the plasters for making me 'hot in the head'.

'You have dimples . . . two on each cheek. Why didn't I notice them before?' I sang into her knee while she was brushing my hair.

'Because I *don't* have dimples,' Tata said, somewhat absently, and added agreeably as if recovering her presence of mind: 'I only get dimples when I'm pregnant.'

On April Fool's Day, Kit flew to Bilibino where we'd be moving at the end of May, two months before Tata would give birth. He phoned the same night and said that our plans had to be changed as he'd been called up urgently to join an experimental team of geologists training to work in space. It was a joke, of course, but Tata's baby turned inside of her, diagonally, as soon as she put the receiver down.

Preparing for our departure, she grew bigger and darker, reminding me at random of the things we'd be lacking in the new place: a hairdresser, any fresh vegetables, a public library, a tailor's shop, spring, summer, streetlights . . . There'd be daily restrictions on drinking water, electricity, use of central heating. No parks or rivers and, for my benefit, no music school.

But I knew we would live in a modern flat (*second* floor) overlooking a range of hills (called 'Love Bites'), with three rooms, a kitchen and a fitted lavatory (although without pipes connected to the sewage system, because there was none). And I heard that the Expedition's newly built office had installed a 'Play Cave' with an ice-cream machine and its own movie projector.

I counted the days to when I'd be off the plane and running for a vanilla ice and the latest cartoons. I remember daydreaming hungrily about the future – with lots of happy endings, every one of them tasting of vanilla.

Eight hundred kilometres north of Seimchan, Bilibino, a small settlement, was established in a bid to increase the productivity of gold mining. This was all due to the repeated history of reports claiming that the area was 'polluted with gold'. Kit himself had witnessed the wonder.

'Gold everywhere, out in the open and the size of a goodish cowpat.'

So Moscow had come up with the idea of building the world's first atomic power station within the Arctic Circle, and signed a memorandum for development of the entire region in the future. The only problem was to find a suitable site for the foundations, for wherever the bulldozers crashed through the frozen earth there was gold flashing back at them.

Since April Tata had worked part-time, spending the rest of her day packing up the contents of the house into plywood boxes, sacks and bags. It would have been much easier, and indeed more practical, to have parcelled up the whole house, securing the windows with sealing wax. She hated to leave behind our one-acre garden, fertile as solid granite, and kept mourning for the outdoor toilet and the cellar, oh the cellar: eight feet deep, the deepest in our street. It had been hollowed out by one of those new 'Arctic' excavators, whose thousand-horsepower jaws minced the eternally frozen earth like garlic crushers. Kit had spirited the machine away from a construction site for a crate of vodka to dig a hole in the courtyard. He was later fined heavily for not having obtained planning permission.

The least we could do about the cellar was to take some memorable pictures of the inside. Our neighbour, a temperamental land surveyor, brought his own camera, hung a paraffin lamp on the wall, and I had to pose, wrapped in Tata's gypsy shawl, surrounded by empty barrels. The neighbour had trouble with the focus; his fingers were going numb.

'Don't breathe,' he said. 'My lens is misting over. It's like an ice-bunker down here.'

I froze, not blinking, as he shouted: 'Look, I didn't say *die*, just don't breathe . . . and smile, will you?'

My only response was to pull up the shawl that was sliding off my shoulders, and this required quite an effort. I was thinking of my father and how he must have felt when, two years before, he had dashed to the cellar to fetch some frozen fish and locked himself in. That hadn't been on a fine day in May with sunny spells and melting snow, but during one of the coldest nights in December when you couldn't work out of doors with machinery because the metal would crack.

At first we thought Kit had popped into the toilet and got carried away. What alerted us was that one of our huskies, Old London, worked himself up into a frenzy, howling, then tried to dig a tunnel down to the cellar, despite the fact that we'd fed him only half an hour before. He's so spoiled, Tata said, and look, goes messing where he fancies, right on the cellar door.

She straddled the broom and dashed out to 'talk' to the dog, only soon she was howling too, calling for help.

If it hadn't been for Old London, Kit would have shared the same fate as the baby mammoth dug out of the steep bank of the Kolyma River. It had been perfectly preserved and therefore (some commented) had the sort of contented, tender expression of the Paschal Lamb. The vegetable pulp in the mammoth's stomach had been as efficiently conserved as the joints of meat stored in our 'ice-bunker'.

Now the cellar was cleared out and Tata was seeking offers, telling everyone how well it had served us. But all the callers asked was how long would it take them to defrost a salami sausage. The neighbour-photographer, who finally got a picture of me in the 'right' mood, did not bother with such questions. He made it absolutely clear we should expect no offers from him.

Tata was peeling some onions, carefully separating their thick brown outer layers.

'What's for dinner?' I asked, kicking my school bag out of the way.

'Onion stew . . .' Tata said, grinning, and placed the onion skins into a zinc bowl that hissed with steaming water.

My mother cooking in the washing-up bowl! I stood by the stove examining her from behind. Well, she was pregnant (you could see it even from the rear), so she must be having her moments.

Tata took off her stockings, straightened one of them and plunged it gently under the boiling onion skins.

'Let's see what happens,' she said. 'Ararat promised me the natural colour of a suntan. These pale stockings make me look anaemic – I want to be bronzed.'

'Pardon?' I hoped I'd misheard her. 'What did you say?'

'I want to be bronze . . .'

'No . . .' I badgered her. '*Who* promised you that?'

Tata threw her eyes sideways, down at me, but lapsed into silence. In this awkward interval I muttered something to the effect of '. . . can't believe it . . .'

'I thought you liked her,' Tata said with a jerk of her head.

'I thought you didn't,' I went on, so fiercely that she forgot her onion 'stew' was overcooking.

Tata stirred her other stockings in and resumed: 'Did you know she's a Taurus? I never get along with them – pushy drones . . . but we talked and I thought, she's only a woman – not that she looks like one, not with a nose like hers . . . and she doesn't really have legs. And her hair – too dark, too woolly . . .'

'Taurus?' My voice faltered – the mere mention of Ararat's name seemed to perturb me since that 'working' night. I had vowed never to go anywhere near her and had succeeded so far. Anyway, Ararat hadn't been seen around lately.

'*Why* did you talk to her?' I finally asked my mother with a rather forced air of superiority.

'She made us an offer,' Tata said, and clapped her hands. 'I've sold her our cellar. She didn't even want to bargain.'

Ararat had called that morning and asked about the price, Tata's health, wishing her well. Oh, how she loved babies, Ararat said; she'd have dozens if she still had her uterus. She'd talked about her health problems and her nomadic life since she'd become a seasonal shepherdess for a multiplying herd of collectivised reindeer. Tata had launched out her sympathy and reduced the original price by 50 per cent – for the missing uterus. Another fifty was deducted for the relief of getting rid of the cellar.

Ararat was so pleased with the deal she'd already brought some things over for storage.

What things? I ran to the cellar and tried the latch, then ran back to the kitchen.

Tata was draining her stockings in the colander. She said she'd told Ararat to put a new lock on the cellar door for 'we can't be responsible now, can we?'

We couldn't, I agreed, forcing my voice to calm down, not even if she left a dead body there.

Tata confronted me with a wide-eyed stare, her face losing its colour. She leaned back on the stool, spread her feet and stroked her belly. I poured her a glass of water, but she declined. Setting herself upright she breathed noisily through her mouth, gobbling air. Her baby must be turning around again, was my immediate suspicion. When I asked her what she wanted me to do to help, she pressed her lips with a finger.

I sat pinching parsley out of the window pots, counting the clock's ticking. On seventy-five my mother shook herself vigorously from head to toe.

She drank some water.

'I was nearly sick,' she said, and drew back, stooping painfully. 'I had to unfocus myself.'

She'd thought about being a white lily, floating in a fresh-water pond. This little trick was known to help pregnant women combat some of their temporary disabilities. In Tata's case this was her excessive intolerance of certain images provoked by simple words like 'body' or 'sausage' – or anything relating to flesh. It had turned her stomach just seeing the deerskin bag which Ararat had brought to store in the cellar.

'I don't think I'll have dinner tonight,' Tata added, and turned lifeless again.

Arranging my bed for the night, I heard a short, warbling whistle roll through the window. I sat pressing the pillow into my knees and waited.

'Koka . . .'

A scratch on the glass, a knock on the pane.

'*Koka-mocha* . . .'

I punched the pillow and turned over to sleep.

Next day, Saturday afternoon, Tata held a tea party in the kitchen. There were two women sitting at the table; one of them was so pregnant that her own husband addressed her as 'Hippo-heap'. The other woman, an Expedition accountant, had been trying to get pregnant since last year. She didn't look like she was enjoying it.

'What am I doing wrong?' the accountant asked, chewing one of our best table napkins.

'Maybe you are trying too hard,' Tata said in her placid, motherly voice. She was busy frying French toast on the stove, which I was summoned to stoke up.

'Don't do *anything* and then it will just happen,' advised the 'Hippo-heap'. She never lifted a finger, she said, and it *did* work.

Still the accountant wouldn't touch her tea. As if by clockwork she was consuming our napkin, staring at the window. She spoke once more before leaving: 'Somebody has broken into your cellar.' It wasn't *our* cellar, Tata returned stiffly and hobbled outside. I followed her, but she sent me back to the kitchen.

The women were getting slowly into their overcoats; the 'Hippo-heap' couldn't even see her feet so the accountant tied her laces and pulled her socks up. They shared the same lipstick (Kremlin Red), painting their lips from memory. I escorted them to the door.

In the hall Tata was talking to Ararat, who slunk back covering her face with her sleeve when the women passed by. 'The new owner of the cellar . . .' Tata performed a brief ceremony of introduction.

'Haven't we seen you somewhere before?' asked the 'Hippo-heap' wearily.

The accountant was genuinely intrigued: 'I thought you were a *burglar*,' she greeted Ararat and hurried out.

Ararat wore a deerskin boot on one foot and a galosh on the other; she was limping. Her face was crusty and peeling. She'd lost an earring and a front tooth, which left her smiling like an old hag, a wicked, penetrating grin. I pretended I hardly knew her. She showed no great enthusiasm at meeting me either. As we entered the kitchen she flopped down on the chair and eyed Tata with desperate apprehension. I stood next to my mother in the pose of a professional meddler.

'So what is it?' Tata asked, giving off an air of discomfort.

'I don't know how to tell you this . . .' Ararat started.

'You *don't* want our cellar . . .' Tata chose the worst option.

'No, not really,' Ararat agreed obediently: she didn't want the cellar.

'But you came here yesterday and *bought* it!' my mother cried.

Rubbing the leg wearing the galosh, Ararat said: 'I came yesterday to *talk* to you – but I couldn't.' She'd ended up buying a cellar instead.

'Wh-what do you want from me?' Tata asked, bristling.

Ararat checked her with a look: 'You have been a blood donor, haven't you?'

Tata bobbed her head.

'You've saved people's lives . . .'

Tata looked distraught. 'I am pregnant!' she insisted, and glued herself to my side.

Ararat turned to me: 'Why don't you go and play the piano?'

I hesitated.

143

'See you in a minute,' my mother said and pushed me through the door.

Half an hour later I heard Tata locking herself in the washroom. I went to the kitchen as if to have a drink, in fact, to remind her of my existence and to check on Ararat. Loathing the idea of reconciliation I put on my best 'impenetrable' appearance.

Ararat was asleep with her head lying on the table, her mouth open, a dribbling gap in a red face. Tata walked in and pulled me back out through the hall to the washroom.

'Now, hold it,' she said, handling me an empty sauerkraut jar. 'Would you pee in there, please – you might save somebody's life . . .'

Later Tata said that even the sauerkraut jar would have had more sense of humour than I had. It was only a mild exaggeration: the minute she put forward her proposal I fell into a stupor, my eyes popping.

On the whole what I remembered then was her persuading me to join some 'underground' humanitarian venture run singly by Ararat. Her funds were limited so in her search for donations she'd come to my mother.

'I don't want your money or your blood,' she'd stated in the course of revealing her mission. She simply asked Tata to be a pee-donor. 'You won't be running short of it,' she had added discerningly. 'Not in your condition.'

Tata was thrilled: she loved donating parts of herself without any structural loss. I reckoned she was longing for a new donor badge, something like 'A Queen of Urine', written

144

in calligraphy. She soon lost all her squeamishness when talking about urine, as if marketing it as a commercial venture: the water of life, a divine nectar, our own precious medicine.

She professed this creed throughout the evening to familiarise me with some salient facts.

Once when she was 'young and silly' she'd sat on a wasp's nest. Her bottom and hands had swellings the size of light bulbs, so Grandma bathed her in urine, collected by everyone in the family, and two days later she was well enough to ride a horse at a canter.

' "Share your *water* with your neighbour when he's in need." ' Tata echoed Ararat's slogan in a high-pitched voice as we were doing the washing up, and pressurised me for another donation.

I squeezed out half a glass.

'You've got to do better than that,' Tata said with enterprising spirit. 'We have a difficult case on our hands.'

'Is somebody dying?' I asked, by way of conversation.

'Not yet,' Tata said, and frowned as if something were troubling her thoughts. We finished drying the dishes in an uncomfortable silence.

After all the pots and pans were returned to their hooks, she suggested a final cup of tea and, although I really didn't want any, she told me to sit down and prepare to receive some important information. *Confidential*, she stressed, lowering her voice. She drew the kitchen curtains and shut the front door.

'Let's say,' she resumed, 'that there was an accidental fire that set light to a Chukchi house . . .'

145

'*Yaranga?*' I put in.

'Yes . . . and this *yaranga* was full of people and children, with Ararat visiting them . . . Fortunately they were all saved, but a girl of twelve – '

'Like me?'

'Yes, a little girl, Lelel . . .'

She had suffered: her back and legs were badly singed. She was taken to the local hospital in Susuman where the doctors talked a lot but couldn't do much. That's what Ararat had claimed, herself a victim of some sinister burns. She had tried to put the fire out with nothing but her foot. She'd been treated in the same ward ('the burns unit') and comforted Lelel who was terrified of doctors and wouldn't touch hospital food – well, who could blame her? Seeing her fading away, her mother pleaded with the doctors to give her Lelel back to the family.

As a refund towards the medical assistance two reindeer were slaughtered and the spirits were won over with the sacrifice of a husky. But the answer was 'No'. Lelel's mother was bundled out of the hospital and not allowed to visit. Naturally Ararat took the woman's side, and by way of expressing her views on the matter she had verbally abused one of the senior members of the staff.

Then followed the abduction, conducted by the girl's adopted brother, a full-time deer herdsman.

They parted in the Kolyma woods, for the boy had to round up his scattering herd, leaving Ararat in charge of his sick sister. Covered in blisters and raw pus, Lelel smelled of tainted meat, poaching in pain. Ararat tore her earring through the lobe, which calmed her down, and began to apply the power of Nature as extolled by the Chukchi, the practice of self-cure for all ills at all times. She treated her own burns with the same universal medicine prescribed to the girl.

'Poor child!' my mother faltered. 'She must be so brave . . .'

I asked what exactly does Ararat *do* to the girl.

'*Waters* her . . . ' Tata told me plainly. She stood up and squatted over the chair, corkscrewing her torso.

'Ararat pees on her?'

Tata nodded, blushing. 'The *waterfall* must carry on . . . ' she said steadfastly. 'We are making it flow '

Lel had a dream.

It was a cold night and the wind, the Big Walkie-Wuddle, took the yaranga down. Lel was crying, aching. The boggy-moss shook, frightened. The toadstool said to her: move, I don't want to lose my head to your left buttock.

Lonely Lel ran like a frightened marten till the Big Walkie-Waddle bridled her by her plaits.

She staggered, sad. Her breasts hardened, hid under her armpits. A star fell down: then another, burning Lel's feet. She cried. A deer came and stood by her side. The Big Walkie-Waddle laughed, howling, and blew him out of the way. The deer twirled like a skewer and flew high. Higher than the moon. Voices were calling him up. The Polar Star spun round him and let him in. He thudded down.

'*E'tking,*' Lel says – a bad dream – and crawls backwards into the *yaranga*. Ararat calls after her, waits, then shouts in Chukchi, a long-range tirade, as if laying out the devil.

We are sitting in a sunny spot on dry, sooty pebbles.

Kolyma's bank, where Ararat and Lel are camping, is damp and crumbling away; the marshy field there is not even camouflaged. Normally, I wouldn't be allowed to come near the place: it's off the beaten track, an hour's walk from the settlement, but I make it here every morning.

There's a colony of cedar trees blocking the only visible access to the *yaranga*. When it's windy the paws of the furry evergreen trees reach to the *yaranga*'s walls and beat them with the assiduity of a country housewife banging dust from a carpet.

Deerskins, stretched around a set of poles crossed at the top, are old and bleached by sun and frost. Ararat boasts she could auction off this compact tundra lodging '. . . anywhere in no time. A small skin-womb for small and skinny people.'

Needless to say, I've never been asked in, although Tata advised me not to wait for an invitation but just go inside.

This last week of May is the Spring Benefit, then comes summer – or so the Trade Union calendar says. Splattered with drifting mud, the Kolyma goes brawling by; the crows, learning to sing, soar down the river.

We would have tea and a tin of 'Deer's tongue in jelly' after the nursing hour. Ararat has to change the dressings on her foot and give Lel's blisters a hard time. She asks me to prepare a smoking concoction of fir needles, the anti-ammonia deodorant which uplifts the atmosphere in our 'burns unit'.

Ararat gets on with her foot; I scorch the cedar paws above the campfire. Where the smoke clings to one side, from the riverbank to the woods, Ararat sets up her operating table, a sleeping bag under layers of muslin. She wears a long woollen coat over a boy's worn-out track-suit.

Taking her bandages off, Ararat swears in all the languages she speaks. Her hair falls loose, disordering a procedure that would put the most experienced nurse to the test – or, maybe, to flight.

She talks to her blisters: to the 'pinkies' (the healed ones) and the 'gruesome greens'.

'Don't be so sure of yourself,' she tells her Boy-toy (the big toe) that is resisting the prospect of new skin. She dunks Boy-toy in a saucepan and splashes him with warm urine.

Every morning for a fortnight the 'burns unit' gets three litres of our 'water'. It travels up in two hot-water bottles and a small rubber ring filled up to the stopper. Without these rubber vessels, vows Ararat, her nomad life as a trainee shepherdess would be seriously impoverished. (I know what she means: *bottles* break, they leak . . . She knows what I know.)

I wear the rubber ring over my shoulder and carry the hot-water bottles in a shopping bag.

Making and delivering 'water' for 'your neighbour in need' leaves little else to live for. I can't concentrate at school, trying simultaneously to control my bladder and relax my brain cells.

'Too much thinking detracts from the urine's quality,' Tata theorises. It gets acid.

We are not rivals on the production line, but my mother's

149

output could be neatly compared to a 'spring tide' effect. Pity we don't have a hose long enough to connect our house with the *yaranga*. This would also serve my purposes, for it wears me out being a pack animal every day. Nevertheless, the urine is well shaken and frothy.

'You're a born delivery man,' Ararat once mumbled in my ear, the only reminder of our somewhat awkward past encounter that was ever mentioned between us.

I can't be sure how this remedy works, but Ararat says it's as simple and as complicated as Nature herself. She seeks a cure, not theories: 'doctors' sick-talk to cripples and crocks'.

She listens to what Lel has to say for the girl sees dreams which become a sober reality within days, even hours. Lel warned her mother, Little Wall-Eye, about fire on the night the *yaranga* burned down. She saw her skin 'changing', rolling off her back like water.

'Give me *your* water . . . ' she'd asked Ararat after Little Wall-Eye was thrown out of the hospital.

She told Ararat what to do. There was nobody else in their ward so Ararat skipped over to Lel's bed and helped her crawl out from the dried-out gauze covers. With her burnt foot raised up, she positioned herself above the girl's body and peed liberally over the red leathery patches.

Although their escape from the hospital was not prefig-ured in Lel's dreams, she'd had a vision of a Russian doll – the one with smaller duplicates inside, each making water to be consumed *off the premises*.

Ararat gave this a moment of serene thought and identified Tata as the big Mummy-doll, the carrier of at least one
little daughter ('You *are* having another girl,' she assured
my mother); then she had followed her own instincts by
recruiting Tata and me as her 'magic fluid' donor team.

One third of all communal 'waters', including her own,
Ararat spends on bathing the 'gruesome-greens' and
smoothing the 'pinkies' with compresses and poultices.
What is left over goes into the savings bank. Old urine
whitens gold, Ararat claims. The smell of it would kill a
python, I say. However, this brooding infusion sets Lel
budding with new skin, leaving no trace of a scar.

She has a special oilcloth tube in the shape of a sleeping-
bag, in which she gets soaked twice a day with most of the
'waters' we produce.

The oilcloth and the blankets, insulating the tube, were
'rented' from the hospital and, according to Ararat, no
patient recovering from burns would be sent home without
a spare roll of muslin. On account of that she'd laid hold of a
month's supply of surgical dressings (enough for the entire
hospital) but still complains she was cheated of her share. If
they had fled in winter, using a 'double' sledge to whisk them
away, she would probably have loaded it up with beds,
bedpans, a bathtub, rubber mattresses and a couple of
nurses to complete her own field '*lazaret*'.

But it was thawing then; spring was galloping ahead of
them. They fled astride a buck reindeer with Lel lying on her
stomach across its back like a pack-load. She bit at her fists,
wrung her tresses, but didn't cry.

Her mother did, left alone in the woods. She wouldn't be

151

seen dead riding a reindeer: Chukchi women were not supposed to trample man or beast – *she* walked.

'Still walking . . . ' Ararat says through teeth gnawing at the pipe she's lighting. Her foot, muffled up with a fresh dressing, rests on her bended knee.

'Maybe she got lost?' I think out loud.

'Chukchi *don't* . . . ' Ararat brays like a prancing donkey. 'They get dead . . .'

She'd expected Little Wall-Eye to be her right hand. The woman used to look after a big family, and knew how to fish and hunt. She spoke some Russian and could bake *kaw-kaw* (bread) on an oil wick.

Lel speaks only to Ararat – and then not every day. Sometimes she cries or sings (neither of us is sure which) and puts herself into a trance – a lethargic sleep that once lasted for two days.

Ararat told me a tale, which gave me a feeling of pure celestial wonder: Little Wall-Eye was in love with Crescent, who was hooked to the moon by his belly-button. It placed him in a very uncertain position, so he asked Dawn-the-Redbreast, to whom he was betrothed, to send Little Wall-Eye his best wishes. Soon she was in labour with twins – two daughters: Lel and her sister, who died in infancy in her sleep.

Lel sleeps now day and night, and eats when she feels hungry – mostly at dawn, if Ararat is willing to respond to her demands. The reindeer that brought them to the crumbly bank is almost eaten, except for his lungs and bowels, the *dead body* Ararat left in our cellar.

I stoke up the campfire; Ararat dozes with her eyes wide open. The smoke screen seems to absorb her pained expression. Her 'shift' has only just started but she is already tired. It's time to pack Lel into her tube. I don't help which is accepted without a quibble.

Lel's name in Chukchi means dewdrop, far-fetched on its own, but it suits her (Ararat says) more as a nickname, for she is small and round. Maybe so, I don't know. I've only seen the girl's head – cinnamon tresses, chalky teeth – poking out of the *yaranga*. A burlesque ferret, sly and soundlessly curious.

She lies on her chest and crawls to and fro with the support of her chin. Her hands have been tied to her hips for being so impatient with the pain and itching. The 'healing itch' is a welcome sign, Ararat repeats as often as she smacks down her own hands thirsty for scratching.

'She won't let me touch her,' Ararat says, returning from the *yaranga*. Her voice is colourless, a stale murmur that stupefies me chilly.

Lel had a bad dream: she'd been bridled. Her breasts hardened, hid under her armpits. She was afraid of Kele, the spirits coming to tame her. Luckily she'd already built a barricade: rubbed her chin to the bone and drawn a blood circle around herself.

'Couldn't she just spit on them?' I ask, tightening all over at the thought. (Well, my grandma would . . .) 'Or call for us?'

'Don't be too clever.' Ararat stomps her foot to halt the conversation.

'Have you ever seen a Kele?' I urge her in a whisper.

153

'Yes,' she whispers back in mock alarm and points her finger at me.

'No, really.' I shift closer to her. 'Do you believe in spirits?'

No, of course not, Ararat retorts. She believes neither in God (she crosses her heart), nor in spirits (she spits three times over her left shoulder).

Before I leave, she makes up her mind: it's time to break off our 'pissing treaty'. Yes, she says, no more 'water', please. She may have to raise some more blood though – to fence round herself and Lel if Kele keeps running amuck.

'. . . Know the donor?' she asks, toying with her ear, torn through the lobe.

NINE

···

THAT NIGHT THE river rose above flood level, to the delight of
the waterworks men who had made their predictions public
two weeks before. Swollen with authority they went on
broadcasting warning messages round the clock. The picnic
area along the forest stream, my starting point for the trips
to the crumbly bank, was proclaimed 'Exposed to Flood
Hazard' and fenced off.

I was stuck. Whether there was another way to reach
Ararat (somewhere roundabout, some side-track passing
by the marshy fields) I hardly had time to discover, for she
soon found a way to contact us. The very day after we parted
a parcel arrived from her: a leathery cloth sack tied to our
front door handle.

'We are leaving tomorrow,' I read her note aloud, 'with a
deer convoy. Lel's mother is here, returning thanks to you.
Find enclosed – a reindeer tooth, which one day brings you
twenty head of deer, the Knights of the Wild Stags. Not to be
collectivised, she said. Please honour this herd. The Black
Raven included will keep you safe under his wing wherever
you are . . .'

'That's all we need,' Tata said, poking her finger at the
ground-off incisor with a long conical root. I investigated the
contents of a smaller pack. There was what looked like a

fusty handful of lucky charms, selected with some imagination: a strip of leather, the skeleton of a cedar cone, half a cork, a button on a sinew, a fur tassel – all bound to a pair of bird's claws, dead stiff. This must be the 'Black Raven', we guessed, or whatever's left of him.

'I haven't been told where we're going and, believe me, I don't want to know . . . ' Ararat had scribbled on the inside of the wrapping paper. 'I miss you . . . We must meet again soon. Until then we wish you a pleasant journey, and easy pushing – to whom it may concern. You are looked after, Lel says. She had a dream: a mackerel sky and an ice floe under full sail. A good sign . . .'

'That's enough!' Tata interrupted me, her mouth curved in a grimace. 'I've got the picture.'

'You mean you know how to read dreams?' I gasped in admiration.

'Well, yes,' she said, a stark wondering attention coming into her eyes. 'If you see a spider you'll get a letter . . . a dog's mess – it's always good news, or money . . .'

'What about *bridling*?' I demanded.

'. . . Doesn't sound promising.'

I jumped up and spun round the kitchen. Tata focused her eyes on me: 'Will you *please* sit, you're making me dizzy.'

I sank down at the far end of the table.

'What is it now?' she snapped.

'Lel had a dream – a bad dream . . .' I started, exhaling, 'she was bridled . . .'

'Oh no . . .' Tata fanned me away as if I were a fly. 'I said *leave* it, didn't I?'

Her face was tense, her lips knotted. Unfastening the top

of her shirt, she wrenched at the buttons as though they were chickens' heads. Oh well, it's all over, she said. Our charges are gone. Now we're moving too, dusting Seimchan off our feet.

'Wet nurses' Tata called us and laughed, shaking her belly. I smiled thinly, trying to match her mood.

'What shall we call the baby?' she purred, regaining my attention.

She was hoping for a girl: 'Victoria or Margarita?' – my mother's weakness for fashion, like having a chignon bun on top of her head, or owning a *Sputnik*, the latest model of vacuum cleaner.

I folded up Ararat's letter and put the Black Raven back in the sack. Tata snorted with relief, almost smiled, but her smile was progressively refashioned into a frown as she watched. I cupped the sack in my hands. How did it get here? I thought, perhaps aloud, for Tata shrieked, swearing under her breath.

I ran through Ararat's letter again – there was no ending in the usual sense. The last sentence, which read, 'Please pack that meat from the cellar and any tins . . . ' finished abruptly where the wrapping paper had got torn. I checked the scraps, every piece, but none would fit the missing bit.

'Have you lost something?' Tata quizzed me, immeasurably sarcastic.

'She asks us to pack meat and tins, but what for?' I asked, avoiding meeting her eyes.

Tata shoved herself back from the table and, radiating waves of disappointment, ticked me off sharply: 'You are not listening to me, are you?'

She reached for her glasses.

'And look at me when I'm talking to you.' She armoured her eyes with the glasses. '*Let all that go*, I said . . . or I'll call your father right away and tell him everything.'

My mother always wanted me to be afraid of my father because, she believed, he was afraid of me. She would order him to tell me off, then stand between us and tell him off for not telling me off properly.

Rebuttoning her shirt, she proceeded in a distinctly lowered voice: 'Would *you* be a proud father having a daughter like you?'

I knew what was coming next – last term's report, a sort of multiplication of indictments: missed school, did no homework for weeks, picked her nose until it bled when asked to explain a simple theorem, daydreamed during the headmistress's speech at assembly . . .

Tata drew breath: 'And *she*, her majesty, lives to complain . . . phones up and goes rattling on, piercing my ears . . . But I kept you out of *this*, didn't I? Said we are moving, not an easy time – so you're distracted . . . Said I'm pregnant and our dog got run over.'

'He never!' somebody said, walking straight in through the hall. 'Isn't your Old London out there romping with my Kukla?' The district nurse, who visited Tata once a week, was usually accompanied by her puppy, a spitz, presently outside and charging London full tilt.

Looking my mother up and down, the nurse established a prime case of hypertension and sent me out to join the dogs.

I ran to the park, and from there by the short cut down to the river. It was flooding, swollen with mud, driftwood wrestling with the current. On the radio, broadcast full volume from the waterworks tower, a brass band played the Funeral March – so slowly as if it was breathing its last.

A crack shot of lightning flashed across the sky, which burst like a rain-filled bag. I sat under a tree on a bench half-occupied by a dating couple. When their kissing came to a halt the woman, young and gaudy, repainted her lips and asked via a hand-mirror if someone ('he', she said) had stood me up. No, I replied, shifting to the far end of the bench. The woman moved to my side and softly squeezed my elbow.

'Gone!' banged the brass band with a clash of cymbals. 'Fin-fin-finish . . .' the trumpets moaned. I came apart, blubbering: 'My friends are leaving, but I can't see them off, what do I do?'

'Whatever you do, don't drown yourself,' the woman said. 'Wish I had your problems . . .' her companion added, fumbling with his fly.

Later that night my father cancelled his weekly call – or rather he wired a short message instead: 'Have to move stop two horses broke loose stop be good my little foxy.'

Actually the last word should have read 'fossil' (his pet name for Tata) but the radio operator who received the telegram either didn't hear it right or made his own correction, assuming that with Mother's reddish hair she was a natural 'foxy'.

Despite the soothing terms of endearment Tata panicked, gripped by bizarre visions of disaster. 'Why did the horses break loose?' she nagged the operator, till his wife interfered and, trying to be helpful, imagined what might have happened: 'Wolves, or some silly shooting in the air or both . . .'

I stayed calm, thinking rationally, watching Tata become increasingly restive.

She kept phoning the radio operator until around midnight. There was still no news from my father. I heard her sighs, deep gut-moanings like voices in the wall settling for the night. The house filled with sounds dissolving in the dark, the bare windows taking the shape of the sky. The door to my bedroom slid away, mingled with the shadows; sleep breathed into my face.

When my mother spoke again her voice was coming from just under the ceiling. Standing on the stool she was rummaging through the cardboard boxes and sacks piled on top of the wardrobe. Wake up, she said, and asked whether I knew where we kept that shoe box with our dressing-up paper hats and masks.

If my mother were a stranger I'd seen looking for a masquerade outfit at three o'clock in the morning I would have thought her rather suspect in the head.

'Got you!' said the suspect in the head, dashing a shoe box down onto my bed. There she sat, slumped, recovering her breath, her maternity shirt flopping over her belly.

She told me to get up and dress: 'Lel's mother is here.'

I zoomed out of bed like a flare.

'Nothing's *happened* . . .' Tata grunted. 'They need food for the road, as Ararat said in her letter. We should pack that meat left in the cellar and some tins – anything *tinned* will do.

'Now just listen.' Tata stared at me sightlessly, her mouth slipping lop-sidedly. 'Don't be surprised, you've already met her, you know . . . I mean we *all* met before. Oh God . . .'

In an effort to calm herself down she pressed her hand over her heart: 'I never thought I would see *her* again.'

'*Who?*' I cried, my mouth falling open.

'The thing is . . .' Tata began, preoccupied though she was, 'Lel's mother is Eichin – that was her name *then*, little Eichin, always hungry for buttons . . .'

She pointed out I was wearing my first tailor-made dress back-to-front. I didn't remember putting it on. *Eichin is Lel's mother* – I racked my brain trying to make sense of this.

I'd heard about Eichin: 'When you were born I was stitched up by a reindeer . . .' My mother had once spun a yarn, a likely story – only it was as true as God in Heaven, she insisted.

It had been Eichin who shared her tundra paraphernalia with *tanechkin*, an outsider, in this good cause. She'd been a new mother herself: her twins, both daughters, were delivered in the same passenger lounge where my mother had me.

As the story goes, the 'wonder thread' brought about two miracles – my mother's recovery, and her friendship with Eichin.

To this day Tata likes to think her life was saved by the nameless wisdom of a primitive culture. In gratitude she showered Eichin with buttons . . .

'She'll just die for a button,' Tata said, emptying the contents of the shoe box onto her lap.

I used to wonder sometimes where they'd gone – our party

hats and masks, all handmade, decorated lavishly with buttons and beads, bright glassy droplets which Tata was now engaged in plucking out, one by one. I stood watching her, beam-straight, still completely dumbfounded.

She told me to make haste to see Eichin and fetch the meat from the cellar. We didn't have the whole night, she went on, showing no signs herself of being pressed for time. She ventured an excuse: 'I need to be alone, just for a little while.' I had a feeling that this encounter with the past wasn't easy for her to bear.

As I was leaving the bedroom she hissed at my back: 'Not in those slippers, for God's sake . . .'

The kitchen door had been left open. I did some extra shoe-tapping to make my entrance resound, and walked straight into a naked body smoking a pipe.

Eichin was sitting on the floor, her eyes closed, her legs spread like a pair of compasses. I could see the reflection of her genitals in the polished toe of my shoes.

When Tata had heard the rapping on her bedroom window she was taken with a terrible thought: this must be a caller bringing bad news about Kit. She'd groped her way towards the front door, breathless, panicking, beyond helping herself. Eichin had to lend her a shoulder before thumping her down on a chair in the kitchen, where they talked.

She was Lel's mother, Eichin explained; she had come in the morning and left a parcel at our door.

She tore her clothes off and threw them on the floor. They were wet, she said, like the waters of the river she crossed that day.

It had been a hard day. She couldn't find the tinned food Ararat had asked her to buy in the shop. The liquor kiosk was closed. A gang of stray dogs chased her up into a tree, where she perched until night fell.

Listening to her, watching her, my mother became overloaded with suspicions that this woman wasn't a total stranger to her. Eichin confirmed her thoughts: 'So Lel says . . . you meet you, you *know* me . . .'

She spoke basic Russian, obviously learned by ear, not familiar with gender or tenses as we understood them. Mainly she expressed herself in the present: short sentences in a peculiar word order invariably beginning with 'So Lel says . . .' like a magic chant, preceding the rest.

After I brought up the deer leftovers from the cellar and helped her with packing, she complimented me by saying, 'So Lel says . . . you *big* . . . Lel *little* – still dewdrop.'

Herself merely a runt, Eichin had a thin, skimpy body, flat chest, hardly any pubic hair. Her skin, although tight and unwrinkled, matched the colour of cooked giblets. She wore her hair in a plait on one side with a tufted lock that, like a pirate's patch, shielded her left eye, the wall eye. It appeared she was painfully conscious about her cataract: 'Kele's evil *spit*,' she explained to Tata.

While I'd been asleep (evidently for the best part of this unexpected visit) my mother quizzed Eichin on her life story, which was reiterated for me later over breakfast with much gusto, an occasional tear and a swear word or two.

Perfectly venal by Tata's definition, these 'neo-swears' were borrowed from Eichin's vocabulary, a coarse version of a nursery primer. In fact, she had learned her Russian at a

163

boarding school in Magadan where her daughters were taken into care. She was accepted there too as a live-in cleaner, an arrangement made by the midwife Fedor Fedorich.

Always generous with money and gifts, he visited Eichin, spoiling the twins. He promised her that one day she and her daughters would return to their roots, set up a proper family with enough deer to clothe and feed them all. Looking for a suitable man to marry Eichin, he once matched her with a herdsman whose first wife, an elderly woman, was very keen to splice her husband onto a younger wife and get herself a maid, but she was dead against having the twins to live with them.

The rejection was like an old wives' curse, an open invitation to the spirits – the wicked ones, the mischief-makers. They went on dogging Eichin's every step, gave her a cataract, then took one baby daughter away. Tricking Kele, she changed her name, became Little Wall-Eye, moved to a hostel, lived there with the night guard – an amputee who, being devoted to his birch crutch, fondled certain fantasies about its hearty application to Eichin. As a result she had ribs broken, an elbow put out of joint, her head cracked open, but there was one notable consolation to weigh in the balance: the spirits didn't hound her any more. The mere sight of the crutch made them cut and run.

When Lel was four, she and Eichin went to a ski resort where older children from the school were taken to see winter sports. There were some Chukchi herdsmen there with families, invited to demonstrate their traditional games. One Chukchi woman recognised Eichin, claiming they'd known each other since childhood. *Yes*, she said, Eichin and her daughter could stay with her. The next morning they found themselves sledge-driven, back on the road that bound them to their land and people, with a hope born of a fresh start.

Wriggling her bare hips, Eichin squatted over the buttons scattered on the floor. She droned on, hushed, and shoved one button, a glassy, scaly cyst, in her mouth. She rolled it about like candy.

'You see,' my mother said, giggling. 'She just loves buttons. So easy to please.'

Eichin *was* pleased, ecstatic rather. There was no point pretending I hadn't seen her rubbing her genitals with a button, moss-green, the size of a ripe gooseberry, which she inserted inside her vagina without a thought.

'Well,' my mother observed to me, 'she won't choke on *that* one.'

Eichin rose and made a rapid swirl, twisted her hips, skipped and jumped. 'Sit in here,' she grunted with satisfaction. 'Nobody knows you here.' She'd hidden her button, we guessed, in a safe place: turn her upside down and it would stay there intact – under lock and key.

'Why?' Tata asked Eichin, breaking the spell, having some difficulty in forming the question.

'So Lel says. . . ' Eichin started, puckering her lips, then broke out vehemently: she wasn't allowed to keep any buttons as lucky charms or to wear beads, nor could she decorate her clothes. If she did Lel would cut every button and tassel off and feed them to the fire. For, she said, her mother wasn't worth it: 'Mother not live like Chukchi, live like *tanechkin*, Mother no good.'

'That's so cruel. . . ' Tata panted.

Eichin nodded exaggeratedly and intensified her complaints about how cruelly she was treated by her only daughter. Lel was rude, suspicious and helped her with nothing. She spoke Russian to her and Chukchi to Ararat. 'Ararat *tanechkin*, want live like Chukchi, Ararat good.'

Tata mulled all this over and asked Eichin when she'd first met Ararat. Eichin straightened up, crossing her legs. She spoke in sound bites: 'Me live with man, man live with Ararat, all sleep in bed, man like Eichin best.'

'What – all in one bed?' I intervened, causing my mother to choke on air.

'Why don't you go and change?' she growled at me, seemingly back in command of herself. 'Don't you think you're a little bit overdressed?' she added in a righteous tone, her gaze travelling from Eichin's bare toes to my flaunting shoes.

She could have told me to leave the room, I thought, walking out of the kitchen demonstratively slowly, then slamming the door.

The dawn light blued the top of the hills; the wind quietened, breezing silently through the windowpanes. Somewhere a wood chopper challenged his axe; someone's alarm clock went off, muffling the radio time-signals.

Changing into my slippers, I paused in front of the hall mirror. I watched myself – the *other* me, who arched her eyebrow, staring at me with a loathsome grimace. I could

166

hear the thoughts the other me was thinking: 'Look at you, sourface. Feeling sorry yourself, aren't you? You've been cheated! I warned you. So what do you think about your Lel now? Your celestial wonder! . . . Sleepwalking, dream-talking, fighting with Kele . . . She's just a girl like you, born in the same passenger lounge. So much for the mystery.'

Tata appeared at the kitchen door, letting Eichin, now dressed, into the hall. Festooned with string bags and sacks, she was preparing to leave.

'Life's so full of *magic*,' my mother bubbled. 'Isn't it magic that we all met like this?'

Eichin squinted, swinging her head sideways. 'So Lel says . . . go see button woman.'

'That *is* magic!' Tata whispered and clapped her hands.

'That is a *lie*,' said the other me bitterly.

Taken aback, Eichin pulled a long face. 'Lel dream . . .' she droned. 'Lel talk to Kele . . .'

'There is no Kele!' the other me raved. 'Lel is a dream-liar!'

'Don't talk to her like that!' my mother shouted, pulling Eichin to the front door.

The other me took after them, pranced in front of Eichin, stopping her from running.

'Lel dreams bad . . . Kele make Lel sick,' Eichin cried, dropping her bags into a puddle.

'Lel is spoiled, she should be told off!' the other me screeched in my mother's voice.

Eichin turned round and dashed away across the yard. Leaving the other me behind I picked up her bags and ran after her, splashing through the puddles, the mud, the dog mess – in my slippers.

....

TEN

BILIBINO WAS overcrowded with builders: men and women, mostly men, dressed in identical black padded overalls and matching tops seemingly all of one size, to fit an Olympic weight lifter.

The builders' headquarters, a secluded dingy barracks, casually ill-proportioned, attracted everyone's eye with an illuminated sign up on stilts, towering above the roof: 'Bloom, the town of our future!'

Actually, in the media and among the higher ranks, Bilibino was known as no less than the capital of the new Klondyke. This was a mild term for the quality and amount of gold that had been discovered in the region of the Northern Anuisk range since the Fifties. As my father said, Anuisk gold was way beyond compare with Alaskan hoard-strikes.

And there was more to come, so much more that the Ministry became panic-stricken and had to revise its current plans up to the approaching Seventies. Their strategy was to wind down prospecting, while spurring on the mining. By and large, however, mining equals miners – and their families. All needed to be housed and fed or fed and housed. Which brings us back to the builders; they were building a miners' town, not forgetting about themselves and the working class in general. Those who didn't fit this category (including gold prospectors) were assumed to be grateful for anything that came their way. But then again, as my father said, the times had changed: *we* were outnumbered and overworked. There was enough gold already mapped to give the miners and their Ministry a splitting headache wondering how to get it all out of the ground before the next millennium.

Thus, being employed to work for the future, we failed – in the eyes of the community – to justify our everyday expenses and were living out of everyone else's pockets. Such a situation, when our very presence felt like a burden, fostered a candid resentment which was displayed to us on far too many occasions.

When we first came to Bilibino, settling in our new flat (on Miners Avenue), Tata received an anonymous letter declaring that by 'occupying' this property we had jumped the housing queue and left two miners' families (children under five, invalid grandmother) to rot in a bug-infested hovel.

The same night at supper a stone was thrown through the kitchen window; the following morning our door could be identified by the freshly piled excreta on the step.

Later in the autumn the Expedition made a request to book the Glitter café for a private party, and was refused without a single valid excuse. Not to mention that we were the only tenants in the house whose firewood supply kept being stolen or delivered to the wrong address.

'Should have packed up and gone.' Tata had counted her regrets ever since, because we stayed on. My sister Vika was born; Kit was recommended for a package trip to the yoghurt region of Bulgaria. I got nits. 'From the *miners'* school!' my mother would rave, whenever recalling this affliction.

Tata went back to work part-time, leaving Vika, packed in with her rag doll and supply of nappies, with a childminder. Katya was Ukrainian, a single mother and unemployed, though she boasted a degree in structural engineering. There was anything but a shortage of builders in Bilibino, so Katya had to wait for a vacancy to join the team of her fellow-countrymen who had been recruited to build 'Atomka', Bilibino's nuclear power station. They were only digging the foundations, but the regional publicity about the 'working atom for the Arctic Sahara' took over the world news and sport. The first nuclear 'shocks' were promised in five to seven years, marking a beginning of a new era for this 'harsh, godforsaken land'.

After lessons I was often summoned to a shift at the school's workshop experimenting with modern craft and technology. The idea was to build a cardboard model of Bilibino in the nuclear age as it was designed by Moscow architects: a Northern paradise with heated glass roofs, productive conservatories, artificial hot springs and happy valleys of amusements.

Because none of us had much experience with model-making, we voted to gain some elementary skills by first depicting Bilibino as built, before tackling its nuclear infant.

We started with the town centre: the triangle of streets, each claiming to be the main avenue, at the bottom of a spreading hollow. The houses (after several conflicting accounts their average number came to fifty) replicated each other – two-storey 'boxes', all painted white. There were no outskirts to speak of, except for the sets of wooden barracks, a shapeless, grimy lot, some clustered at the backyard of the centre, others providing fencing for the airport runway. Bilibino ended at a jumble of burned larch trees, carbonised toothpicks, rising up the slope of Burnt Hill.

We ran out of cardboard, and equally of enthusiasm, threading the shuttle bus route to the mines, up and down the hills and off into nowhere, where these multiplying units were nestled in the plainer surroundings of the tundra. Being told to keep their location 'strictly discreet' we did a good job of camouflaging the mines with stacks of moss, passing for trees, and scabs of semolina, faking snow. Fools we were not, to let a state secret leak out from a too-perfect scale model.

October, 1963, Saturday morning. Fritters fizzling in a frying pan. Steamy windows, drooling windowpanes.

It's been almost a month since Kit returned home from the field, but Vika thinks nothing of him, and whips his whiskery kisses methodically with her fists.

Wc breakfast in the living room; Kit sits with his feet resting on the chair and mulls over his life. He nearly lost his right foot this summer when, completing a one-man trek through an intractable region, he slipped off a cliff. His pickaxe had fallen down the side of the gorge, while his foot, trapped in a crevice, had saved him.

It took him hours to free himself, and there he was, half-consumed by mosquitoes, his leg gone numb up to his knee.

Three days later he was found in the woods, crawling to his staging-post on all fours.

Tata makes him up a hot mustard bath in the tub, which she puts under the table so he can soak his feet. He groans and moans, screwing up his eyes. I let him finish off my fritters.

When the table is cleared of dishes, he rubs his feet with seal fat while composing an outline for my first *anonimka* – an anonymous letter to *Pravda*.

All of us, he says, at least once in our lifetime, write or think of writing an *anonimka* (a standard denunciation or satire) to a newspaper. It is as natural as losing your milk teeth or falling in love.

Pravda, Kit reckons – just like every other newspaper, however small – thrives on anonymous letters. So-called 'straightforward' correspondence from readers who willingly identify themselves is somehow less trusted and has to be double-checked before even being considered for publication. *Anonimkas*, on the contrary, are first published and then checked – and only then if there's enough of a public uproar.

It would be a real treat, my father thinks, for an adult newspaper like *Pravda* to get a letter from 'a child, preferably a boy, physically fit, doing well at school, who writes an *anonimka* on a dead man'.

Kit offers no explanation of what all this is about; he has a hot flicker in his eyes that pleads. I guess he is bursting to say something publicly, to make his ideas manifest in print, but doesn't know how better to do it than by using my *anonimka* as his mouthpiece.

172

He wants me to be 'outraged', and tells me how I am to feel as a boy, 'an outraged Boris', the son of a gold prospector. I start with the essentials of any *anonimka* – a plea to help right a wrong.

Like his father, Boris has a life model, Yuri Bilibin, now dead but once a living legend. Bilibin had fought his way through ministerial mazes to the Chukotka gold fields where his prospecting team made the first big strike of the Kolyma empire.

That was in 1928 – now history, a thing of the past. Bilibin, too, is long gone and turned to dust. He'd rushed to nonentity without leaving a single plaster bust behind. He'd lacked the vanity to be photographed or painted for posterity. There are no memoirs written by him and his field diaries outline work routines only. It's not surprising that the place named after him keeps no memorabilia of his life and nobody here bothers to honour his birthday or mark his death.

'Blast.' Kit, reading over my shoulder, pounds his fist into the table. I stop writing.

'How shall I put it?' I ask casually.

'No. *Boris* . . .' he grunts, despairingly, 'it's all wrong!'

'Write it yourself then!' I snap – now I am outraged. I was quite pleased with the result – a full page written in my best calligraphy.

'I did write,' Kit says, not grumpy but somewhat rattled, 'but I couldn't get past *Pravda*'s pen-rats . . .'

He calls for Tata and asks her to bring a 'hundred grams' to tickle his spirit. He downs his measure and gives a short gasp. Ah, went down well! He closes his eyes and recites

173

some verses: 'Prospecting these days is yesterday's story –
the front page is kept for the miner's glory . . .'

'Who wrote that?' I ask, seizing an appropriate pause. Kit
raps his chest, grinning, and reads more.

It sounds like an average-length poem of a sardonic
nature, which he wants to see in broad circulation but, so
far, no newspaper, including *Pravda*, where he sent it, has
supported or even acknowledged his efforts.

'They're done with us, *Boris* . . . ' he adds, hitting his fists
together, and then rhymes incoherently, 'Gold to gold, dust
to dust . . .'

I lean towards him, recharging him with a stare. I have an
idea. I ask him: would he like me to cast a bust of him? I
could arrange this in our workshop – we do make models
there, after all.

Kit unlocks his fists, picks at his beard. 'Put me on the
list,' he says with a taunting smile. 'How do you like me in
profile?'

On the eve of my parents' wedding anniversary, which fell on
Revolution Day, the 7th of November, Tata applied herself to
the traditional festive chores. Cooking took up most of her
time: we expected guests for the following night; then there
was ironing to be done and after that Kit remembered that
his special 'banqueting' shirt needed a fresh starching.

It was getting close to midnight but she was still on her
feet, sweeping the communal stairs.

The two-storey house where we lived contained four flats
on each floor. Previously our flat had been divided into three
separate bed-sits with a shared kitchen. It was a comfort-

174

able apartment: centrally heated, spacious and quiet. Dressed in leather with a personal mail-box painted red, my bedroom door opened into the passage leading to the entrance. I could sneak in and out without being noticed or even heard.

Checking on my presence, my parents would strike a hammer on the central heating pipe in their quarters and wait for my reply. They lived on the 'far side', next to the kitchen; their door sported a bell and a green mail-box. There was a hole in my bedroom wall, down at floor-level where the central heating pipe ran through to our living room. Originally discovered by my sister (her head once got trapped in there) the hole-in-the-wall became an irreplaceable aid in the art of eavesdropping.

My parents seemed to suspect nothing of the sort; otherwise they wouldn't have been arguing or making love in the living room. And it was there our phone was reinstalled following my mother's demand for greater privacy. I must have overheard her most confidential revelations of the decade. I just couldn't help it: my ears spent so much time stuck to the hole they grew addicted to it.

That night I took Ozhigov's glossary to bed. Reading dictionaries was my mother's idea of self-education. Her expectations for my future had shrunk since, in her words, I'd started 'incubating' amongst the miners' children. Every fortnight she gave me a spelling test on a list of random words that were particularly barbaric to the tongue and grammatically treacherous.

At present I was forging my way through the letter 'D' – from 'dithyrambic' to 'Donquixotean' – fraught with difficulties, when Kit answered the phone. It was a long-distance call for Tata. 'Ararat's on the line!' he shouted, waking up Vika who cried in a frenzy.

My mother cried too: 'I was thinking about you! Why did you stop writing?'

Her correspondence with Ararat was one-sided. We received her letters but couldn't reply because there was no return address. Ararat seemed to have been ceaselessly on the move since the summer we parted.

This July, a few days before my sister's first birthday, Ararat had phoned from a miners' settlement which was only three hundred kilometres south of Bilibino. She was well and happy, she said, 'camping with the herdsmen'. Lel lived with her, but Eichin had returned 'home' – to her adopted son Vaal and his uncle, both herdsmen working for a collective reindeer farm in the area. Ararat was seeking employment there too, and her main news this time spoke for itself: she'd got a job.

'A radio operator? *You?*' my mother bleated into the receiver.

The line wasn't always clear, so to avoid misunderstanding she kept repeating what Ararat was telling her. Thus I gathered that Ararat had some 'domestic' problem on her hands – as if anything could be considered 'domestic' in her haphazard nomadic life.

She complained about Lel 'being difficult' and cursed the 'devils' – Vaal and his uncle, who couldn't stop fighting with each other and had to be split up. Now the uncle was leaving for Uelen, probably running for his life.

'Book him a flight . . .' my mother started to make notes,

echoing Ararat word for word, 'to Uelen. Two weeks from now . . .'

'Of course he can stay with us!' she added cheerfully, carrying on writing down names and the address – some fishing village on the Bering Strait where she would have to send a telegram to the old man's relatives so someone could meet him at Uelen's airport. There was a long pause while my mother listened to Ararat, then she asked: 'Did you *live* with him?' – a touch of embarrassment in her voice.

She might have guessed what the answer would be.

'Of course, I shouldn't have asked. . . ' Tata remarked, offhandedly. For some time she went quiet, droning an occasional *Oh, yes* or *Ah-ha* while I rested my right ear, setting my left one to work.

'He did . . . he did . . . *that* to you?' Tata resumed, her voice faltering. 'I can't wait to see him . . .'

She stamped her foot in excitement, chuckled.

'Oh, it's *him*!' Tata butted in. 'Uncle the herdsman – I've heard a lot about him . . . yes, from Eichin. Yes, I know *how* you met Eichin . . .'

Oh, *him*, I thought, *that* herdsman – I remembered him too. Well, what Eichin had said about him. She once moved in with a man who'd apparently been living with Ararat which wasn't a problem since they all slept together.

My father's irritated whisper burst in from the corridor: 'Do you know what *time* it is?'

Tata hushed her voice, saying it was Kit sending his regards. She was about to put the receiver down when it occurred to her that she'd missed the herdsman's full name. She took down the details, spelling each word slowly. His surname was Laagert'eeg, pronounced Lagatik. His other name was spelled T'eu Leen.

'Say it again,' asked Tata, concentrating. 'Oh, that's nice and easy – *Teulin* . . .'

'*Teulin!*' I howled down the hole. It echoed back, booming, exalting the quiet. '*Eetti* . . .'

My parents' anniversary party was a success: the guests didn't leave till four in the morning. One man, who arrived in the middle of dinner, played the harmonica for the rest of the night – anything you asked him. Nobody knew who he was.

That night I was left in charge of eight children, two dogs and a newcomer – the Expedition boss's daughter, called Cornelia. She was my age, but looked older because of her oversized glasses, bicycle-like, wire-rimmed. She talked little, bit her nails. Her favourite colour was red, her favourite pet a cat. She couldn't remember having dreams or secrets. She was apathetic about God or Kele.

I was desperate to make friends with her.

It felt safe just to be around her, shy, content, her head wagging like a china Buddha, her glasses sliding down her nose. I would push them up for her and she'd steam up the lenses gasping her words of gratitude. Passive by nature, she was born to be trouble-free. That was the nicest thing about Cornelia – she would never get you in a scrape.

We sat at the same desk at school and did homework together. I wrote her book précis while she went crawling after my sister. They talked to each other in a language that no one else understood.

'Aren't you lucky to have Cornelia?' my mother once said.

178

'She's the perfect answer for a best friend. Just think, who else would want her? Nobody. She's all yours. No competition or rivalry. No secrets lost.'

My mother went as far as saying that Cornelia was to me what Ararat had become to her.

I spent a night at Cornelia's, then another; we slept on a folding sofa, feet to head. I read to her my diary – selectively, from particular pages written in code. It was a kind of *ad hoc* statement on my one-night 'delivery service' set up by Ararat in the not-too-distant past. Cornelia sat listening, biting her nails with impressive speed. She reminded me of a starving gerbil. When I turned over the last page, she was chewing the collar of her nightshirt. Sorry, she said, steaming up her glasses, so sorry you lost your father's 'stripey'. As never before it struck me now that Cornelia was a sensitive and caring person. She wanted to know what had happened to Ararat and Teulin, 'if you don't mind me asking . . .' I hoped she would, and launched into telling her the rest.

She looked dismayed, wagging her head as I mentioned that Teulin was coming to stay with us this very weekend. She said nothing, not a word, not even after I'd drawn her an accurate picture of how I felt at the prospect of meeting Teulin again. Maybe I shouldn't have told her everything, I thought, testing her stare, her eyes full of subdued anxiety. It was clearly all too much for her. But after a moment's hesitation I heard myself asking: 'Could I – when he comes – stay here, with you . . . ?'

'Only if you want to,' she said, turning her eyes ceilingward. Then, with a muffled sigh: 'I'll have to ask my mother.'

ELEVEN

....

Teulin was expected to arrive on Friday night, Saturday morning at the latest. As Ararat informed us beforehand, he would be delivered to our door by his nephew Vaal who, in an act of reconciliation, had agreed to supervise the journey. They'd be deer-sledging from one of the herdsmen's camps near Bilibino.

Tata took Friday off, preparing to welcome Teulin 'in style'. She turned my bedroom into a guest room (aired to a minus degree), cooked deer tongue and meatballs – bowls of them arranged on the kitchen table and windowsill.

After school, en route to Cornelia's house, I came home to pick up my sleeping bag. My mother was in the kitchen, brushing the floor while munching a meatball. Of course, who was I to tell her off for transgressing one of the main rules of proper behaviour that she'd taught me: eat at the table and never on foot. She talked to me with a full mouth, giving orders.

Before I left she told me to take a tray of meatballs up to the communal attic. We had a portable 'refrigerator' there: my father's field trunk full of shoe boxes substituting for food compartments.

To reach the attic, I had to go out of our flat to the staircase and climb a ladder. As I went up I heard a thumping noise above my head. The trapdoor shook, shuddering as if under knockdown blows.

'Who's there?' I asked, then listened. The pounding intensified, reinforced with a throaty whining. I dropped the tray at the foot of the ladder and called for my mother.

'Somebody's up in the attic . . . trapped!'

Tata rushed out of the door and leapt onto the ladder. She was scrambling up, shouting, 'Don't panic! We'll get you out of there . . .'

Well, it would've helped if whoever it was up there (must be drunk) would stop kicking the trapdoor. This wasn't the easy way to open it.

'Listen to me!' Tata hollered, balancing on a step. 'Lift it up! By the handle . . . *Up!* It won't come down . . .'

It properly would have if she hadn't been propping it up with the bun on her head. Prepared to overcome any obstacle, she shoved with such force that the trapdoor burst open as though erupting from a blast.

The door landed on top of a body bundled up in furs. We crept around it, plucking at the loose ends, and recovered a head in a padded hood with a shivering tassel at the back.

'Are you . . .' Tata turned the head to face her, 'Teulin? You must be . . . Are you?'

The head nodded, churning its tongue in a mouthpool of blood. He couldn't speak, bless him. I felt better.

Tata clattered down the ladder, rushing to get the First Aid box. Teulin kept groaning. He had bitten his tongue when the trapdoor slammed into him. Choking on Tata's fiingers as she dabbed his tongue with cotton wool, he spat

181

into her apron and moaned. She spoke for him: 'Poor little man, didn't know what he was doing.'

By that time Kit had arrived home from work.

'What was he doing in the attic?' he asked, squatting with me at the edge of the trapdoor.

'Killing time,' Tata replied. She advanced the theory that Teulin must have arrived when she was out and, having nowhere else to go, invited himself into the attic. 'And there he was all alone and lonely. *Weren't* you?'

Teulin crossed his eyes and thrust his tongue in and out: he *was*, poor him.

'Couldn't get down,' Tata went on in a cheerful moan, for how would one know how to open a trapdoor if one had never done it before?

'*Now* we know how, don't we . . . ?' She patted Teulin on the head. He eyed her fondly. So far, he hadn't given me a second look.

'Do *we* know anything about planes?' Kit asked in a mocking voice. 'Have *we* ever flown before?'

'You leave it to me . . .' Tata said with aplomb, and yanked me down the ladder. We had things to do.

I was sent to collect my sister from the child-minder, who'd gone shopping taking Vika with her. I found them queuing outside the bakery that sold boxes of chocolate and puff-pastry 'Napoleons'. Vika was having a tantrum, screaming frantically, and the child-minder had given up on her. When we finally got home, Tata was laying the table for dinner.

Teulin wasn't expected: Kit had offered him some vodka to

rinse his mouth for lack of antiseptic, but he'd swallowed it instead – a good measure, enough to send him asleep.

Tata kept checking on him, running herself out of breath. She was obviously neither fit nor used to negotiating the attic ladder with such frequency. Admiring her efforts, Kit thought of providing her with some practical assistance. He suggested tying a washing line to Teulin's foot; the other end, stretching through an air-vent into our flat, would be attached to Vika's rattle. This 'alarm system', as he called it, would monitor Teulin's every movement and let us know within a split-second if he stirred.

At first Tata rejected Kit's idea, saying it was ridiculous, but on second thoughts (considering the long night ahead and Vika's bad waking routine) she agreed to give it a try.

This was a night that proved an old saying to the letter: you are born to your parents, you don't choose them. I watched mine, their jaws working, their hands with their nipper-like fingers sorting through Vika's toys in search of the biggest, the noisiest rattle of all, that would produce the maximum effect when set in motion. There was no end to their arguments about which room to instal the rattle alarm in, but the washing line (conveniently strung up in the attic, where we dried the linen during the winter) was just about long enough to reach my window directly below an attic vent. The rattle was put onto an extension lead and drawn into my bedroom. It was 'just handy' as Tata said, overruling my vague protest.

So I was delegated to keep a watch on Teulin and never made it to Cornelia's. She phoned me but only talked to my mother who sent my apologies, saying that I would be available tomorrow.

I'd gone to bed with my diary, turning over in my mind what we'd planned to do that evening at Cornelia's: learning to hula-hoop, watching their home movie 'Cornelia Is Dying'. When Cornelia was seven years old she was run over by a drunk motorist. She'd been in intensive care for weeks, not expected to last long. Her father then borrowed a movie camera and filmed every moment of his daughter's life embracing death – until one night she opened her eyes and quite clearly imitated the voice of her favourite radio nanny: '*Little bully-bull jumped to the moon. Silly little fool.*'

It was five in the morning. Teulin was off the washing line, jumpy as a rabbit, calling my name.

Kit woke me up.

'He doesn't know my name . . .' I said, dry in the mouth.

'He's calling for Koka, can't you hear?' Kit whispered. 'Ask him what he wants, he won't tell me . . .'

I chained my feet round the bedstead's bars. My father's voice was becoming hoarse with aggravation, but then trailed away.

Teulin had vanished. There was no sign of him anywhere, in the attic or downstairs, but he'd managed to shut our door the right way.

'He'll be back,' my father promised, tucking in my blanket. 'You'll talk to him – won't you?'

I chose not to think about this eventuality, hoping by then to have evaporated in a cold sweat.

The rattle alarm was withdrawn from my room, the

washing line returned to the attic. For breakfast I had a scoop of snow off the windowpane and a cluster of icicles that I crunched at as if they'd been stolen.

Good, I thought, clutching my throat, my tonsils will be mushrooming any minute, choking me to death.

Teulin was arrested walking a reindeer across the airport runway. He was taken for questioning to the control tower, to the very top, where he felt so dizzy he had to be blindfolded. The operators thought they'd caught a Chukchi who'd got lost on the way to camp, but Teulin, being cooperative in his limited Russian, assured them it was his deer who had brought him there.

Elgar was his name, a *talking* reindeer. He *told* Teulin that he'd only seen a plane from below ('above his horns') and asked if he could have a closer look at one on the ground. That's why the two of them had ended up on the runway doing a bit of peeping.

After Elgar's wishes were satisfied (for he couldn't wait to be tied up to a telegraph pole), one of the air traffic controllers, Gorelko, walked Teulin back to our house.

Although we hadn't been acquainted with Gorelko personally, he was a well-known man in the settlement. None of the calendar 'red days' would be celebrated without him giving talks about his life. Once, dressed in his wartime uniform, jingling with medals, he came to our school assembly. I wrote in my diary: 'Gorelko is such a nice man, cries easily.' He had been a fighter pilot in the war and flew King Cobras to the Front. That was when the Americans wanted us to beat the 'Fritzes' and sent their gift-planes to

Seimchan. He made some good friends among the Allies. He took one of them to meet the Chukchis and this American traded a cigarette lighter for a pair of deer horns . . .

Teulin liked Gorelko. By his own modest estimation, Gorelko must have done the right thing: after the questioning he shared his tobacco with Teulin and greeted him in Chukchi – '*Eetti.*' They understood each other, speaking a word in Russian, two in Chukchi and the rest by gestures. Moreover Gorelko was *ring'etvitkul'in* – a pilot in Chukchi, a word to remember.

'You fly high,' Teulin courted Gorelko, windmilling his arms to show how high – as high as you can get, reaching the land of the spirits, the Polar Star.

They walked with measured steps through our yard, then peed behind the firewood fence before smoking a pipe together on the porch. Here, Teulin gestured to Gorelko, here his friends lived, a Russian family, whom he described in one word: Koka.

He was relying on Koka to look after his reindeer while he'd be away. It wouldn't be too long before he'd come back but his Elgar wasn't the sort of deer to be dumped with a collectivised herd: he was used to personal care.

'He's gentle as a puppy . . . ' Gorelko cried out loud, setting the glasses in our kitchen cupboard clinking. Tata refilled his mug with vodka; her hands were shaking.

'You've got yourself a pet, Koka,' Gorelko went on, his eyes collecting tears, 'a full-sized deer.'

Tata looked at him as if he had taken leave of his senses.

'She's not an animal lover,' my mother snarled and signalled me to get on with my tea.

She herself hadn't eaten since morning, when Teulin went missing. Only half an hour ago she was ready to set up a rescue operation, planning to call out our neighbours and friends to go off on foot. She'd bolted downstairs to the Serpovs' to ask for help and found Gorelko and Teulin sitting on the porch side-by-side, like two cooing doves.

She'd yanked Teulin's arm and he, at the sight of her, grunting, her eyes like daggers, had sprung up and darted off to the attic. Gorelko – his face flushed with excitement – had no objection 'to pop in for a chat over a glass of something hot, and plenty of it'.

'It' went into his mug and loosened his tongue. Once again we realised that there were no deals with Ararat, however small, that couldn't go wrong in a big way. Whatever she was involved with, problems came naturally.

Aiming her words at Gorelko, my mother murmured: 'You see, we've got instructions. I wrote them down, it's very clear: book Teulin a ticket – a return ticket – and see him off on the plane, that's all! No pet deer!'

'Maybe Ararat forgot to tell you,' Gorelko soothed.

'Maybe,' my mother groaned as if she'd suffered a mild concussion. 'Only I think I was set up.'

I knew the feeling.

Kit trotted into the kitchen with a plate of reheated meatballs. 'He hates this,' he said grinning, 'and he wouldn't talk to me.'

'He can talk *like* you. He can copy anyone,' Gorelko began, using his words carefully; by now his tongue had little power to obey him. 'He said you didn't like him . . . sh-sh-shouted and n-nagged him about some *doors* – "pushit pullit" . . .'

'I didn't nag him!' my father said defensively.

'But he likes *you*, Kok-ka,' Gorelko winked at me, spilling genuine laughter. I was doing the washing up; dropped a plate.

Gorelko jumped up; his eyes became focused at once.

'Have you heard him speaking from his belly?' he cried. 'He can throw his voice . . . make anything sound like it's alive.'

'We *will*.' My mother leaned towards him, petting his arm, anxious to return to her concerns. 'Do you know when he's coming back?'

Gorelko winked, concentrating. 'Soon,' he replied, looking over his shoulder as if to make sure that no one was there, eavesdropping on him. 'Gets his tambourine and "off – home", that's what he said.'

'What?' my mother bleated. '*What* did he say?'

That he was going to visit his relatives who are coastal Chukchi from the Bering Strait and live in a fishermen's village near Uelen.

He was born there and brought up by his older brother who was the village's head shaman. Last year Teulin's brother had died and left him a 'moonface' tambourine, bequeathing him, so to speak, his major tool.

'A *tambourine*?' my mother asked, hardly audible. 'I got myself into *all this*,' she muttered, her eyes growing round, 'because of a tambourine!'

'. . . and a beater,' Gorelko whispered, glancing over his shoulder again. 'A smooth-tongued beater . . . It beats the hell out of imps and angels. I think that's what he told me.'

'Why?' my mother groaned, as if asking for mercy.

Gorelko, however, interpreted her question in his own way.

'Because the old man is simple, believes in superstitions,' he blurted out, stammering. 'I mean, he really thinks that if he could *tambourine* his wishes to something – somewhere – up there, it'd take care of him . . .

'*Tram-boom-boom, tram-bam!*' he roared and jumped up. Clapping one hand over his empty mug, he tapped his feet, moving in seesaw motion. My father joined him, banging the saucepan lid with the scoop.

'Two fools!' my mother said, bristling, and went off to talk to Teulin.

According to Bilibino airport regulations the ticket, which was booked in advance, had to be collected not later than forty-eight hours before departure.

Later that afternoon, Tata suggested that before doing our weekend shopping we should go to the ticket office. There was a small queue, mostly *them* –

'Miners,' Tata commented, whispering to me as we stood in line.

Sitting behind a glass screen with a small window the cashier was friendly and polite. She spread Teulin's ticket out on the counter to show that everything was in order: to/ from Uelen, Monday 8:15 am, a window seat at the front.

Tata was already emptying her purse when the cashier tapped her fingers on the glass and asked to see the passenger's passport.

'Passport?' Tata surveyed the cashier with a puzzled frown. 'But he's a *Chukchi* – I don't think he's got a passport . . .'

'Then he can't have a ticket,' said the cashier censoriously. It couldn't be validated without the passenger's passport number, his date of birth and a *propiska* – his residential permit.

'*Propiska?*' Tata cried out. 'I tell you he's a *Chukchi*, he lives out there, in the tundra . . .'

'He's a herdsman,' I confirmed, addressing the queue.

The queue was getting impatient.

'Does he have a birth certificate?' asked the miner standing behind Tata.

'Where would he register his birth?' Tata asked him sternly. 'They're born as they live – *camping*.'

'They do,' I confirmed, dismissively.

The queue was becoming agitated; complaints were breaking out from head to tail.

'What I was going to say was . . . ' the miner raised his voice, 'if you don't have a birth certificate, you can't apply for a passport.'

Tata slammed the shopping bag on the floor. The cashier smiled weakly at her. 'And I'm saying,' she said, brushing Teulin's ticket off the counter: 'No passport – no ticket.'

Tata pushed me to the end of the queue and told me to stay in line and wait for her.

Half an hour later the ticket office was empty. I was supporting the wall under the scrutiny of the cashier.

The phone rang. She answered, sighing, listened and took some notes.

'Do you want a sweet?' she asked me, having one herself. Cherry Candy. When did I last have a Cherry Candy, I thought, turning away from the glass screen.

Finally Gorelko, greased in oily sweat, appeared hand-in-hand with my mother. 'Let us in, please,' he said to the cashier, 'I've walked my legs off . . .'

After we were seated, Gorelko performed a short introduction: 'Our Lilichka,' Gorelko caressed the cashier with his eyes, 'looking younger every day.'

Lilichka blushed and straightened her stockings under the desk.

'Now, let us have a ticket,' Gorelko prompted her bluntly.

'But I can't, Pavel Petrovich,' Lilichka said, gaping at Gorelko. 'I've got my instructions, and the rules are . . .'

'There is no such thing as a rule that can't be broken,' Gorelko stated firmly.

Throwing back her head, the cashier let out a girlish sob. I felt sorry for her: her face looked kind in profile, and it was so nice of her to offer me a Cherry Candy.

'Lilichka,' Gorelko urged her, 'let us have a ticket – *please*!'

'But Pavel Petrovich,' Lilichka said, collecting herself, 'there's very strict passport control in Uelen, it's a sensitive area there, on the coast, you know . . .'

'Know what?' Gorelko asked, challenging her.

'The frontier . . . the Americans are just around the corner.'

191

'Americans, you say,' Gorelko nodded, falling into a momentary stupor. 'During the war,' he resumed dreamily, 'I worked with Americans. I mean we worked together. Are they still there?'

'They must be,' Lilichka said, fumbling with Teulin's ticket.

'I've heard them on the radio,' Tata intoned.

'Me too!' I said, to say something.

Gorelko wiped his eyes with his uniform sleeve.

'That was the time, my friends . . .' He breathed out his starting phrase, which had been circulating through all his public talks for special occasions. He reviewed our faces with the kind of detachment a conductor would assume calling for the musicians' attention. Delivered in a voice used to speech-making, his familiar lecture sped by, each recollection brightening his dreamy expression.

He'd seen America on many occasions when escorting the Allied ferry planes, flying from Alaska to Seimchan. He flew above Little Diomede Island, the last American land in the Bering Strait, some fifty kilometres off the Russian coast, straight over Uelen. The 'Little Dime' (and on a clear day it did look like a rusty coin framed in a chunk of ice) drifted alongside its Russian twin, the Big Diomede – 'Big Dima' – only four kilometres away. If it wasn't for the open waters and the stream of ice floes, Gorelko reckoned, 'we'd be in walking distance of the Yanks.'

'That's what I mean!' glowered the cashier. 'They are everywhere.'

Gorelko relaxed his forehead. 'Lilichka,' he droned on,

reaching for her hand, 'won't you trust an old pilot like me?'
The cashier crinkled her eyebrows, looking aside.

'Well then,' Gorelko said, 'give us the ticket. I promise you
this ticket is as safe as its owner. He would never go
anywhere near America.'

'What are you talking about, Pavel Petrovich?' The cashier
interrupted him nervously. 'I thought an old pilot like you
would know that without a passport nobody can get anywhere *near* Uelen.'

She paused while Tata clawed my knee under the desk.

'You won't even be allowed to leave the plane if you don't
have a passport . . .' Lilichka concluded with *that* look, the
knowing one.

Gorelko ran his hand over his face. There was a momentary silence, a turbulent minute or two, before he said: 'He's
not just anybody, Teulin, you know, he's a Chukchi, an old
man who could be your grandfather.'

The cashier told him she wasn't short of grandfathers,
had a full set of them and grandmothers too.

'Well, good for you!' Gorelko cried out. 'Not everyone's so
lucky . . . Some of us haven't a single relative left alive!'

Gorelko was speaking for himself: his entire family had
died in some siege or air raid, another well-talked-about war
drama in his life.

I don't know why, but I felt dangerously excited as I said:
'Teulin's brother died and left him a tambourine.'

The cashier looked confused; regarding Tata blankly, she
asked in a murmur: 'This passenger of yours . . . Teulin . . .
Is he going to a family funeral?'

Though she sounded wondering, the submessage in her

voice suggested there might be, after all, a way out of our predicament.

Tata searched Gorelko with a conspiring stare. I didn't know what she had in mind, but one thing I was certain of – Teulin's brother didn't die yesterday. This appeared to be irrelevant in view of the circumstances.

Gorelko squinted at the cashier and shook his head. 'The old man lost his only brother,' he wailed. Tata sighed. I forced out a moan. I was learning fast.

'Why didn't you . . . ? Couldn't you have told me right away?' Floundering for words the cashier clasped the phone and dialled a number. She talked to her superior, the croaking voice in the receiver – a Major Tumanyan – who seemed to be on close terms with her and generally the kind of man to deal with an emergency. In our case it was 'a frontier funeral to be attended by a passenger whose passport's out of order' as the cashier put it. After passing his 'deepest condolences' to friends of the deceased, Major Tumanyan expressed his wish to see Tata and Gorelko in person: 'with *their* passports, please'. Conveniently his office was placed (or rather hidden) in an extension to the airport's warehouse.

While I ran home to fetch Tata's passport, Teulin's ticket was set in order. It was issued with an additional slip compensating for the lack of an identity card. Handwritten by the cashier, it stated that Teulin Laagert'eeg was approximately 55–60 years old, born in Uelen and had a temporary residence permit in Bilibino at our address. Secured with Tata's and Gorelko's passport numbers, the 'identity slip' was authorised by a triangular stamp from the Major's pocket.

He was pleased with a job well done.

'Better safe than sorry,' he said, tilting his formidable head. Of course, he said, the passport control in Uelen was official and, yes, very strict – but the officers there usually didn't bother with Chukchi that much. They're used to their wickedness: some would apply for passports but then refuse to be photographed. What can you do about it? Bad practice, they say, annoys the spirits. Full stop.

Gorelko was the last to leave the Major's office. He shook his hand, asking through cordially smiling lips if there was anything we could do to show our thanks.

'It's nothing,' Major Tumanyan exclaimed, happy to have his service acknowledged. 'But if he – that passenger of yours . . . coming back . . . might bring some caviar? Red or black.'

'At Uelen,' he blabbed, 'you can get it wholesale from the fishermen. All of them regular poachers . . .'

TWELVE

···

WE HAD THE REST of the weekend to ourselves, letting Teulin hang out with Gorelko till his departure. And after he'd gone at that awkward hour – eight o'clock, Monday morning, which none of us had ever remembered looking forward to – we were belching with joy all through our delayed, stand-up breakfast. By supper we missed him. It didn't do much for our appetite. We sat in silence, marinating ourselves in what seemed to be an everlasting concoction of guilt and regrets.

Our regrets were numerous, particularly on my part, for I couldn't help thinking that I'd known him longer than almost anyone else, yet treated him as a complete and undesirable stranger. Although I'd stopped avoiding him and once encouraged some unpretentious conversation between us, I should at least have reassured him that he was leaving Elgar in safe hands. Gorelko had offered to take charge of him, and Teulin reluctantly agreed. It was clear I wasn't seeking any contact with Elgar nor wished to learn the rudiments of 'deer-care' as Gorelko did under Teulin's supervision.

Teulin was an enthusiastic herdsman, full of tricks and ingenuity. He had trained Elgar to be fastidious in his choice of food. Moss or lichen spoiled by human footprints (rather than Chukchi's), or by anything on wheels, was ousted from Elgar's diet.

That morning when he double-crossed the rattle alarm and suddenly disappeared, Teulin made one of his trips to the 'hill-over-the-hill' to stock up on Elgar's forage. He wouldn't take Elgar with him ('Old deer, need rest' was his excuse). He brought him meals on a plate: mini-stacks of virgin lichen seasoned with moss and snow-encrusted shreds of bark. All Elgar had to do was nibble until chock-full.

'You might just as well chew it for him,' Kit mocked Teulin at the first opportunity because he felt the old man resented him for no apparent reason.

'What have I done to him?' he kept grumbling.

It was some time after Teulin left when one night, returning home from the public bathhouse, Kit found the answer: 'He hates me for *invading*.'

'Nobody hates you.' Tata soothed him with a kiss before adding offhandedly: 'We are only doing our job.'

Kit was in no mood to be patronised and an argument ensued.

'We *did* our job,' he snapped. 'We are hardly needed here now – voluntary resignation is preferred, nobody cares what happens to us . . .'

I was putting my mother's hair into rollers. Our eyes met in the mirror, we drew a collective breath.

'. . . or to this land,' Kit proceeded wryly. He ran his fingers through his beard, pulled it, plucked it and came out with a germ of a slogan: 'But once it's *used*, it's left as waste.'

Tata protested: he was exaggerating surely.

'Surely,' Kit interrupted her, 'it's waste if a deer has to be trained like a dog not to pick up filth provided by us. That's what we're leaving behind with gratitude for the *golden* years . . . and what comes next?' he asked, pondering. 'Listed pastures? Lichen rations?'

And so he went on, prospecting for the aftermath of his 'invasion' in the name of progress.

I progressed to the back of Tata's head where I used the last roller. We had some spare ones kept in a kitchen drawer. In my absence she moved from her dressing table to Kit's lap. He groaned good-naturedly as she rocked her rollers on his shoulder.

'Teu-Teu-lin,' she drawled, 'we should have . . . Oh, I don't know – treated him better . . . why didn't we?'

'It's never too late,' Kit murmured, conversing with her rollers. 'We'll give him a party when he comes back. Let's have Elgar as a special guest.'

I'd look after Elgar, I promised.

I'd look after Teulin, promised Kit.

We would *tambourine* our wishes, Tata said. Teulin would speak from his belly.

Three years before, my mother's Aunt Katerina, a museum curator, had slipped on a wet bathroom floor and broken her hip. It healed the wrong way, making her a cripple entitled to a wheelchair as well as her disability benefit.

'One almost prays for a crisis, as a rule it's beneficial,' Grandma had noted in her letter. After reading it, Tata cracked her fingers nervously and rushed to the post office.

198

She'd always been grateful to Aunt Katerina for taking her in when she was a student and had no place to live in Moscow. What's more, it was Aunt Katerina (herself a spinster) who'd advised her to cross out the one-armed lieutenant as a prospective husband and 'shop for better' in the Far North.

Tata had sent her best wishes and a hundred roubles to prove she meant it. The money was collected by the Jasevitzes, Aunt Katerina's neighbours with whom she shared a communal flat.

Boba and Frida were pensioners, a childless couple with no close relatives in Moscow; they had adopted Aunt Katerina as their only next-of-kin.

Boba had taught her to walk again, using a kitchen stool on which she'd lean for support, and it did make her life more tolerable and independent – at least to some extent.

Then last autumn (it was on one of those mushroom-picking trips to the country) both Jasevitzes were crushed by the 'masses' boarding the last train. The news reached us a few weeks later.

'I walk with the stool, Boba on crutches, Frida goes by the wall . . . ' Aunt Katerina commenced her letter. Tata, in return, sent a 'seasonal bonus' to the afflicted household, augmented by a parcel of high nutrition food: tins of cod's liver and smoked salmon.

Obliged as they were, the Jasevitzes couldn't wait to exercise their gratitude. They advised my parents to get registered at Aunt Katerina's address before, in the event of her death, someone else could move in. The time required for this pressing matter should not be wasted, for Aunt

Katerina was further undermining herself by setting up her funeral arrangements.

'We are too old to start living with new neighbours,' Boba explained in his letter: 'Please come soon and plant your feet . . . to establish your residence.'

Kit always said he'd hate to end up living in a city ('the concrete hive'), and so would Tata, but they didn't mind staking a claim to eighteen square metres of capital property, overlooking the safari park of Moscow City Zoo.

So my parents started planning their winter holiday, a short break in Moscow. They stayed late at the office, clearing their workload before taking their leave. I had to make dinner, feed Vika her 'mashes' and nursery rhymes – the unbeatable combination which would always send her off to sleep.

My parents' dinner was kept warm in their double feather beds. They ate in the kitchen and, if I were passing by, we'd talk.

'How is Elgar?'

'Putting on weight.'

'. . . and Gorelko?'

'Losing weight.'

From my diary:

> *27 November*
> Wednesday, a sanitary day at school. No lessons. A week since Teulin left. Somebody from Uelen sent a telegram to me. Just two words – Teulin came. Our attic still smells of him. Yesterday I met Elgar for the

first time. It was good that Cornelia was with me. On my own I'd never touch him – I'd stand a mile away. Elgar lives inside the airport hangar. It's almost empty. Gorelko cleaned it up and dragged a tree trunk there so Elgar could scratch his back. I don't know much about deer but Elgar is a strange one. The fur on his body looks like it's been whitewashed. Gorelko said that's why he's called Elgar – it's 'white-coat deer' in Chukchi. Elgar's fur is very short and he has bald patches, one round his neck like a skin necklace. He likes to stare at people and if you talk to him he shows his teeth, blinks and sort of hums.

2 December

Our school has been closed since last Friday. It's minus 42. Radio says it will drop lower. Bad time for the outside thermometers. Some of them burst. Cornelia reckons I should get mine a mitten. She keeps her thermometer in her bedroom above the radiator so it's safe all through the winter.

Hula-hooped at Cornelia's. Her father gave us a geography test. He asked us the name of the country where they just shot their President. Cornelia's mother said the Americans think they are better than us, but we send people into space and they shoot their *President* in broad daylight!

3 December

We visited Elgar again. Cornelia brought him sugar lumps and he let her polish his one and a half horns with Vaseline and a velvet cloth. It really changed his appearance, as if he lost ten years. Gorelko told everyone that Teulin won't recognise him, not a chance. I hope he does – otherwise all of us will be in big trouble.

4 December
Gorelko has never looked better. He bragged he's lost ten kilos – not a gram less. He skis every morning to Bridge Valley and hunts there for Elgar's food. He walks him a lot and they run along the runway to keep fit. Gorelko thinks, here in the North, deer should be everyone's best friend as they have been for Chukchi since the hoariest age.

5 December
Gorelko's birthday. He's 49. My mother invited him to dinner. We cooked fish pie with fried sauerkraut and bought a bowl of ice-cream at the back door of the Glitter. Gorelko turned up in his pilot's uniform from the war. He's so old but still handsome. Just balding. Another pilot in my life. I wouldn't mind marrying one some time.

He brought us a weather balloon (he said it was *for the girls*) and some navigators' maps for my father. They shook hands and Gorelko cried a little. He does cry easily. It suits him. We sat and ate and read the maps. They have lines like lace and numbers from top to bottom. I couldn't understand a thing. One map had been torn by a bullet from a dogfight with a

German Fokker. My mother said it was *terrible*. I thought so too. Gorelko cried again and got so upset he couldn't eat any ice-cream.

My father looked at another map and found some spot which he thought was Uelen. He was right, of course, which really pleased Gorelko. He's been in Uelen and knows it well. The town is small and pinned to the coast. Chukchi fishermen and border guards live there. They live and work like one big happy family. The guards' wives brew vodka and trade it for kegs of caviar and seal skins. But that's only between us, Gorelko said.

Gorelko didn't leave until midnight. Every time I was told to go to bed I pretended not to hear, but I didn't miss a word that passed between my father and Gorelko. The maps went straight to their heads and spun them around: the places they talked about wanting to see, the places they would never get to, so near but so far.

'. . . Absurd!' Kit kept repeating, tapping his finger over America. 'It's only walking distance between us, the *heads* of the world, but we don't mix . . . Siamese twins that won't talk to each other.'

Gorelko agreed: 'The Cold War at its freezing point.'

Letting a thoughtful pause settle, I asked how long it takes to walk to America.

'*To walk*'s not the right verb,' Kit corrected me, 'bearing in mind the ocean under your feet . . .'

He was close to adding something, but Gorelko spoke first. He pointed out that walking to America was as possible as getting there by boat. It was a matter of 'hitting the right moment and having a bit of luck'. Once a year for a week to ten days (between December and January) the ocean goes to rest, 'sleeps' as the Chukchi say, then you set off. The American border is less than two hours' walk and, with good company, it's a pleasant and easy journey.

Not batting an eye, Kit seemed to be locked in his thoughts.

'You can *walk* to America,' I said, as Tata soft-shoed into the room, bringing tea.

Gorelko couldn't resist galvanising us further with more revelations. Some time after the war he met a man, a professional soldier, stationed at Uelen. A failed candidate for the Navy, he used to 'drop in and out of the States' on leave, sailing with Eskimo fishermen. That was in summer, during the picnic season, and it *was* as easy as going for a picnic. Not for long though. The season had changed; in came the Fifties. The 'twin heads' turned away from each other and fenced themselves in.

Two great heads with wired-up teeth and ice-shrouded sockets swam side by side in the ocean.

'You don't love me!' cried one head.

'I do,' moaned the other, 'I do love you.'

I woke up. The hole-in-the-wall was illuminated, booming with voices.

My parents were still in the living room – at this hour! Couldn't they find a better time for doing it?

'You don't have to if you don't want,' I heard Tata saying. She sounded disappointed.

'I want to,' Kit said drowsily. 'I was just thinking . . .'

'Oh God . . . ' Tata muttered, sighing.

Kit snapped: 'I am not going to Bulgaria!'

'But you said,' she hollered. 'Didn't you say this to me – I want to travel, I want to see the world . . . ?'

'Not *that* part of the world,' Kit growled. His lighter started clicking and I smelled cigarette smoke. 'I'm not that desperate . . . (no, he wasn't, you could tell by the hollow tone in the hole) . . . to see them and their yoghurt region populated with goatherds.'

There was a bumping sound; fabric rustled then hushed.

'I know what you're thinking,' Tata said, speaking now as if from a distance. I thought I knew too. 'It might be just around the corner, but you can't get there.'

'Then I won't go *anywhere*!' Kit growled between puffs.

By now Teulin had been away for almost five weeks. He kept in touch with Ararat who, consequently, was tipping us off. That's how we knew that he was still 'paying visits', chasing his distant relatives scattered all along the coast.

On New Year's Eve my parents bribed me with a box of fruit jellies to look after Vika and went to a masquerade ball.

'See you next year!' Tata whispered, throwing airy kisses as she ran out of the door.

Huddled in her cot, Vika was already asleep. I moved to my bedroom – seconds before nine o'clock when the Magadan radio station started the festival broadcast. Almost simultaneously our doorbell rang.

I let Ararat in and she hurled herself at me: 'I've made it, Koka, I'm *here*.' Muffled up in a shawl over her sheepskin, she was intoxicated with excitement.

'Where is everyone?'

'At the ball.'

She dropped her sack and pushed the shawl back off her head. 'But I sent you a telegram!' she cried, an undercurrent of hostility in her voice. 'I warned you I was coming!'

'We didn't get any telegram,' I shrugged, thinking: *typical.* That's Ararat for you, nothing will ever change her.

But she looked different, not quite herself. At first I couldn't find anything unusual in her appearance. I tried to reduce my stare by blinking as she shed her coat, yanked off her boots.

In the kitchen while she was unpacking her sack on the table, the ceiling light caught her in its glare, producing a revelation: she wore lipstick; her moustache had gone.

'I left without permission,' she spelled out with an explosive breath, 'just to see you!'

'It's so nice of you,' I reciprocated, catching an apple as it rolled off the table which was becoming overloaded with packs of various shapes and sizes.

'I bought all *this* for you!' Ararat raved at me. 'I *bought* it,' she emphasised and gave me a sharp look.

Something – like a momentary heatwave – stopped me from thanking her. I offered her some fish pie but she frowned and turned away. I excused myself to check on Vika. She followed me to my parents' room and there, at the sight of Vika flashing a smile in her sleep, broke down.

'. . . shouldn't have ever bothered you,' she cried, stumbling back to the kitchen.

'It was no bother,' I said merrily.

'*Him* and his Elgar.' She was panting between sobs. 'Do you think I *knew* what he was planning? Even when he's away I don't have any rest.'

'When is Teulin coming back?' I asked invitingly.

'Never you mind!' Ararat shrilled.

I hummed with as much indifference as I could. She blew her nose.

'We are going to Moscow,' I said.

'Why?' she asked hastily.

'Never you mind!' I returned.

She laughed and set me laughing – and then I challenged her by promising to tell her why we were going to Moscow if she'd tell me when Teulin was coming back.

'I'm not sure . . . not yet,' Ararat moaned. 'Trust me.'

I do, I said doubtfully. We sat on the floor, leaning towards the warm side of the stove. Ararat took my hand and squeezed it, then went on chattering. She must leave tomorrow before getting into *real* trouble with her superior ('hateful man, should be kept in a cage'). Besides, she was expecting a call from Uelen. She had a contact there in the fishermen's co-op where Teulin's relative worked who communicated with her by short-wave radio.

'Did Teulin get his tambourine?' I asked casually.

Ararat shouted with a renewed vigour: 'He got himself a *shaman!*'

All I could find to say was: 'A what?'

'A *who*,' Ararat corrected me; she was talking with a hectic toughness. The tambourine came with a shaman because Teulin didn't claim his inheritance in time and it had changed hands. Now by some unwritten Chukchi law both Teulin and the shaman had equal rights to the tambourine and the beater.

'Is he a real shaman?' I asked.

'They're all real! Let a Chukchi get hold of a tambourine and he will rank himself as a shaman.'

Ararat screwed up her eyes and clenched her fists mannishly. I gave her a light nudge on the shoulder and her face lit up.

'Where's that fish pie?' she asked with a self-pitying smile. I sprung up off the floor.

'. . . and bread. Do you have any?'

She hadn't tasted fresh bread for months, nor butter or even powdered milk. She had deer 'for breakfast and for the rest of the day – every day'.

I topped the fish pie with lumps of bread and butter; Ararat sniffed, wiggling her lips.

She ate slowly, talked fast; the plate that was perched on her knees wobbled. 'Teulin, you know . . . he's just an old man, he's all right,' Ararat was saying, 'it's Lel – do you remember Lel?'

I steadied the plate which was sliding off her knees and nodded.

She tapped her foot soundlessly and went on, revealing a bizarre story that could compete with one of those traditional tales, told appropriately on New Year's Eve.

Last spring Lel was asked to consider an arranged marriage.

Vaal the herdsman, Teulin's nephew, proposed to her in advance with the best of intentions – to secure their future marriage in a traditional Chukchi way. Everything was done properly, within the family. To formalise the agreement they had a ceremonial dinner, during which Vaal laid his cards on the table. First he wanted Lel to go to school (the same boarding school where he went as a child and learned his Russian); then, when Lel was eighteen, they'd get married. The answer that came from Lel was roughly this: it's all very well – but I have had a bad dream.

The guests arrived, but nobody listened to what Lel was saying.

'You know Lel,' was Ararat's remark. 'She lives to dream, she talks dreams, we've heard them before, one too many.'

The next day Elgar had gone for a walk and came back with a broken horn. As Lel had said: she saw a deer in her dream being hurt. 'Kele's work!' she cried. The spirits wanted their offering, a 'fee' for the marriage: Elgar's flesh and bones or no bonds at all.

Teulin had almost had a fit, for he was haunted with fear of losing Elgar. He always believed that Elgar was his soul-spirit. If one of them went it would be the end of the other too.

Frightened as he was, the old man showed fight – there was no way he would give up Elgar and his own life for his nephew's marriage. He threw a punch at Vaal and warned him: leave Lel alone, find yourself another bride. Vaal just teased him and laughed. This terrible squabble went on for months. Finally, Ararat stood between them and told Vaal he had to go away for a while. So they were separated. Peace at last.

209

It lasted for two days, a wisp of time, before Teulin and Lel started going at each other. Though both of them feared Kele they couldn't agree on a way to render them harmless until Lel came up with a solution. It was her idea that Teulin should claim his tambourine and beater to ward off the spirits. He asked Ararat to get him a ticket to Uelen and made it clear he wasn't going to leave Elgar anywhere near Vaal. Elgar was to come with him to Bilibino.

Preparing for his journey, Teulin was in a good mood and even volunteered to be reconciled with his nephew. It was only when they were sledging to Bilibino that Teulin revealed his secret plan. He bragged that he would bring the shaman's voice – the tambourine – and it would put Vaal to sleep. There would be no marriage. His Elgar would be safe.

Vaal was glad to see the back of his uncle. He was busy courting Lel, visiting her as often as he could. He bought her clothes to build up a 'wardrobe' for school. Lel showed her appreciation for Vaal's efforts by drugging herself with sleep.

Her bad dreams returned in a whole kaleidoscope of nightmares, among which was the one that tormented her most since the days when she and Ararat were nursing their burns on the crumbly bank of the Kolyma River. She saw herself being bridled. The wind – the Big Walkie-Waddle – fettered her with her own plaits. She saw a deer, white as a moon, putting his horns, like arms, around her. But the Walkie-Waddle blew him away. The deer flew high, where the voices were calling him, all the way to the Polar Star, the land of the Kele. And he fell straight into their hands.

'I remember that dream!' I said, clutching Ararat's arm. At

once a motion picture stirred in my mind: Ararat changing the dressing on her foot, me fanning the campfire. It disturbed me then, those bridlings and blowings, but that was *then*. Now I could only see Lel as a schoolgirl, learning at gentle thirteen how to read and write.

'Let's not dream over the New Year,' Ararat said, getting up. She rummaged through her sack and brought out a bottle.

'Let's have a drink!' she said, filling two glasses. 'Oh, by the way, what was the name of that man who helped Teulin get the ticket?'

'Tumanyan.'

'Armenian?' she asked, arching her eyebrows.

'I suppose he is.'

'That's useful!' Ararat grinned, raising her glass in a toast. 'I brought something for him – to ensure a smooth landing . . .'

'What landing?'

'Teulin's! I told you he'll be back in a few days.'

Ararat had gone long before I woke up. My parents didn't go to bed at all. After returning from the ball they had continued their celebration with Ararat.

My mother was having her New Year's cigarette when I joined them for breakfast.

' "Bridling" means marriage,' she said, plunging herself into intensive dream analysis. 'Clear as day. The Walkie-Waddle is Vaal – sure he waddles, all Chukchi do, they have bow legs . . .'

211

It could be anyone then, my father objected, but she dismissed his unpretentious logic with a critical grimace.

'The white-as-a-moon deer is Elgar, of course. Poor him . . . There's definitely something nasty about being blown by the wind, but to be called up there by voices – that sounds awful, really bad.'

'It's a kind of warning,' Tata rambled on. 'Some token of bad news.'

'There is no *good* news,' Kit said. 'If Lel doesn't want to marry Vaal, why can't she just tell the truth and sleep happily ever after?'

'You mean . . .' Tata mused half-aloud, then snapped her fingers as though to accelerate her thoughts and broke a thumbnail.

'It hurts,' she managed, after clearing her throat. 'Imagine breaking a horn!'

Kit nudged me, scoffing. 'It hurts telling the truth,' he said, articulating every word. 'Maybe that's what is wrong with Lel. She's afraid of facing life – so she's dozing it away.'

'If you think she's lying, why do her dreams keep coming true?' Tata cried. 'Lel knew two years ago what would happen to her, the marriage, and that a deer – him, Elgar – would be in trouble, the lot!'

'It's Lel who's the problem,' Kit said. 'Can't anyone see this? Where Lel's dreams have driven Teulin?'

'What are we going to do?' asked Tata, biting her thumb.

'*We*,' Kit gazed down at her imperiously. 'Personally I thought *we* were going to Moscow,' he said and left the table.

Tata reached for another cigarette; her chair gave a creak, releasing the silence. I was gulping my cold tea while she studied the bottom of her empty cup, as if trying to break the code of the tea leaves' pattern.

'The shaman's coming for dinner . . . ' she drawled in a small voice.

From my diary:

1 January 1964

I don't want to go to Moscow. I have nothing to wear there, no friends to be with. I miss Cornelia already.

2 January

I met Gorelko in the shop. He was carrying two bags of sugar lumps. For Elgar. I wanted to prepare him. I was going to say guess who's coming back? But he looked at me and started to cry: don't tell me, I know, I know. One of his bags split at the bottom. People were catching sugar lumps for him and he was telling the whole shop that Elgar has to go and he couldn't bear it. I walked him back to his barracks. He held my hand and asked if I could pass Elgar on to Teulin because it would be too hard for him to do it himself.

My mother thinks we shouldn't be involved. No dramas, my father said. Just a party.

They don't think much about the shaman. He's coming in a set with the tambourine and that's all there is to it. I wonder if he'll do some tricks at the party. We could sit Teulin and him as a pair.

These were my school winter holidays, which coincided with

the high point of Vika's potty-training. It kept me out of doors. I was told not to but I slipped out of the house before my mother could make up her mind about how to subjugate me domestically first thing in the morning.

I was out with Cornelia. We went skiing, mastered the hula hoop, did manicures for each other, watched 'Cornelia Is Dying' projected on the kitchen door while Cornelia's father would serve us 'fish stroganoff' or dry potato and rice cakes.

Vaal came on Saturday morning, the day before Teulin and the shaman were expected to arrive. He parked his deer and two sledges on the Burnt Hill and went shopping. In the evening he invited my father out. They managed to jump the queue at the public bathhouse and stayed there until closing time.

The bath attendant, who secretly ran a bar in the men's cloakroom, asked Vaal for his autograph.

'A Chukchi in a bathhouse – hell must be breaking loose!' he said laughing out loud.

Vaal swore at him in more than one word, which my father dared not repeat in front of me.

I noted in my diary: 'Vaal's Russian is so good you wouldn't believe he learned it at boarding school. He likes to do the crosswords and repairs things. He fixed my father's two-way radio and recharged its old batteries.'

On Sunday morning Vaal said, 'Let me handle this . . .' He was to meet Teulin and the shaman so we'd have plenty of time to lay the table and decide who was going to sit where.

'Get ready for twelve-thirty, at the latest . . . ' he stressed, consulting his watch as he left for the airport.

Twelve-thirty became two when I took my position at the window and was the first to see them approaching our house. With a hood shielding his face Teulin tottered on his own. Vaal was waddling arm-in-arm with a man who from the distance looked like Teulin's identical twin, only bigger and somewhat hulking.

'The shaman is coming!' I hollered, bolting into the corridor. Tata ripped off her apron and hopped after me. Pulling his socks up, Kit dived under the coat rack in search of his shoes.

Vaal pushed Teulin and the shaman through the door.

'Lock it!' he said, his slit eyes sharp as razors.

The shaman got jammed between my mother and me. She had overdone it with her perfume, Red Moscow; her lipstick, Kremlin Red, was smeared.

Vaal's chin was jutted out aggressively; he shook Teulin by the hood: 'Tell them who he is, tell them yourself.'

Teulin gazed at the shaman, winced and swivelled his head towards my mother.

'Leutin,' he half-whispered.

'I'm Tata,' she said and bowed to the shaman.

He was breathing heavily; a drop of sweat balanced on the tip of his nose.

'*Water . . .*' he exhaled. '*Water, drink – I want.*'

He said it in clear English. My English teacher, Salomon, would never do it better.

THIRTEEN

··

NOW THERE'S A series of blank shots in my memory, followed by a cinematic rush of scenes. My mother pulls the curtains frantically. Leutin throws himself into the corner of the living room, his thin braid twining over his back. He looks scared but not as much as my father who parts Vaal and Teulin, preventing a fight. Vaal is flailing his arms and shouting. Teulin shouts back. They are shouting in Chukchi. The subtitles are provided in my father's voice: *Teulin walked to America. He had to – his tambourine and beater ended up there. He smuggled them back. He didn't mean to smuggle in the shaman but he had no choice – his tambourine and the shaman came in the same package . . .*

The clock face showed some minutes after 3 pm. Teulin had decamped to my bedroom. The shaman kept himself unapproachable, hidden behind the dining table, where my father's two-way radio was set up for transmission.

Vaal knew Ararat's frequency and caught her in the middle of broadcasting a weather bulletin. He talked to her in Chukchi.

'What's done is done,' Ararat returned quite calmly in Russian, sounding as if she'd received yesterday's news. She surrendered to Vaal's demands and promised to bring

216

Lel as he wanted her 'packed to go to school' within forty-eight hours.

'Don't do anything stupid. Wait until I get there,' she said to my father before claiming with feigned enthusiasm that Leutin was *her* sole responsibility.

Vaal left to take care of his deer shortly after Gorelko rushed in. Trying to get his way, Vaal had frightened my father and Gorelko with the possibility of going to the authorities about Teulin's 'identity slip'. He seized that crinkled, stained piece of paper that we'd had so much trouble obtaining to buy Teulin a ticket to Uelen. It became apparent that the shaman had somehow shared Teulin's 'identity' when flying from Uelen to Bilibino. His name was added (after a comma) in line with Teulin's initials in sloppy handwriting, without the slightest pretence of matching the flourishes of the cashier's lax, curly script.

Who conducted this blatant forgery we would never find out, but it worked out pretty well for the shaman and very much against us. For Leutin, being a Chukchi descendant from Alaska, was provided with, as it was clearly stated at the bottom of the 'identity slip', a temporary permit at *our* address, officially signed and sealed by Major Tumanyan.

Gorelko and my father sat up until the next morning agonising about being involved (at *their* respectable ages) in the shaman-smuggling of the century. Gorelko kept scratching the small of his chest where an itchy spot was budding above his heart. When they ran out of cigarettes Tata occupied herself by making tobacco 'rollers'.

I wasn't encouraged to ask questions or to be seen around. I sat under the coat rack in the hall, ruminating on the letter 'T' from my glossary: *taboo, trapeze, typhoon* . . .

All of us hardly slept or ate for the next two days and nights. The odd callers, including Cornelia, were despatched from the door with vague excuses. Our neighbours (as it was revealed at a later date) thought we'd been 'arrested' by the flu, whereas, in fact, my parents were expecting to be arrested by the militia at any minute.

Every two hours my father or Gorelko went to check on Teulin and the shaman, who were confined to my bedroom with a gallon of water, some cold hot pot and a bucket for a 'pee pot'.

Once I spied on them through the keyhole: they were squatting in the middle of the room, their chests bare, their faces consumed by trance-like stares.

At the end of the second day, as I listened to their raised voices, a whirr of chanting or muttering that stung the quiet of the house, anxiety began to test its power over me. I tried to calm myself by punching at the glossary, pacing up and down the hall. Then, as if being called, I walked into my bedroom. The shaman was on his feet, flapping his arms with a fearful haste. Teulin lay across the room, his eyes rolled up, not blinking, his mouth set like an open sore.

'How are you?' I asked the shaman, my heart making a frog leap into my throat. He sharpened his stare, piercing through me, pinning me to the wall. There I stayed, standing limp, the glossary flopped down over my knees. The room tilted round, shook, then slipped into darkness.

From my diary:

8 January

Ararat and Lel are here. Arrived yesterday at night.
Good timing. The shaman had just put me to sleep.
He and Ararat are held now at Tumanyan's office.
Vaal got Lel. Teulin got nothing. He lost his tambourine to the shaman. My mother said she was glad I was
asleep. Me too. I wouldn't like to have seen what
happened. The shaman just snatched the tambourine out of Teulin's hands and didn't even say sorry.
Ararat was *very* sorry. She told my parents not to
worry but, of course, they did. My mother started to
smoke. My father paced around like a caged bear.
Gorelko scratched himself to bits. Nobody cared
about me.

Vaal returned with Elgar this morning because
Teulin wanted to leave. Vaal is running him by sledge
to the herdsmen's camp. Teulin was so sad when he
left. Vaal was angry. He was going to take Lel to school
but she asked him first to help Teulin get back home.

9 January

News from Ararat. She thinks we are out of trouble!
Tumanyan's *in* it. After all it was *his* stamp on Teulin's
identity slip. Tumanyan's the one worrying now. Also,
his secretary remembers the New Year's presents
that Ararat got for him. And he took them *all.* If only
he'd known what they were really for. Ararat said that
the Major needs her help in Uelen. They must bring

219

the shaman there *immediately*. Gorelko thinks we've been lucky so far but he wants to go to Moscow and talk to his friends from the Aviation Ministry. Just in case something goes wrong. He keeps losing weight.

The next day my parents went to work. As much as they wished to get on with their own life, they decided to cancel their trip to Moscow 'until things settle down'.

That same evening Gorelko called in to report that he'd seen Ararat and the shaman boarding the plane. They were guarded by Tumanyan and his personal aide. After the plane took off Gorelko booked himself a flight to Moscow.

'I'm not running away . . .' I heard him saying apologetically. He was talking to my mother at the door. 'It might be better if I . . .'

She interrupted him: 'When do you leave?'

'On the thirteenth . . .' he said, hesitantly.

Tata sighed. Gorelko muttered to himself.

'Could you get one more ticket?' Tata asked, unnaturally loud. There was an awkward silence before Gorelko's breathing expanded into a nasal titter.

'A seat by the window?' he roared merrily.

Tata pushed the door to my room, opening it wider. 'Well,' she said, meeting my eyes. 'What do you think?'

The plane was half full; we sat at the back with no passengers in front of us. It was a night flight. Gorelko fastened my belt, glanced at his watch.

'Sleep,' he said, lending me his pilot's shoulder. He was taking me to Moscow on a big silver plane.

Feigning sleep I watched him. He slumped back in his seat and closed his eyes. His hair, an untamed grey crop, frizzed at the top of his head. He needed shaving. His shirt could have done with a wash.

His head dropped onto my shoulder, I held my breath unloosening his tie.

After the first stop in Magadan we flew to Khabarovsk. The stewardess's voice peeped out of the radio and woke me up. Gorelko sat upright sniffing the air.

The stewardess started serving Aeroflot breakfasts. When she brought a tray to our seat Gorelko told her we'd already been provided for. He cut a meat pie, sliced some meat loaf – our snacks for the journey.

We had more meat stored in the hand luggage compartment. There must have been half a deer there packed into jars: deer conserves sealed with lard. Four jars were destined for Aunt Katerina and the Jasevitzes; another two were reserved for Gorelko's friends at the Aviation Ministry.

'Eat – eat.' Gorelko nudged me.

'You won't find meat like this in a shop,' he said to the stewardess who accepted his offer to help herself to a slice of meat loaf.

'Where did you find it then?' she asked full-mouthed.

Gorelko winked at me and mumbled: 'It's a long story.'

'We've got a long journey . . .' the stewardess remarked absently, licking her fingers.

Gorelko's eyes strayed towards her legs; he cleared his throat and asked whether she was married.

The meat, in fact, had come from Teulin as a parting gift. Vaal had brought it, the skinned carcass draped over his shoulders, the night after Ararat and the shaman had flown off to Uelen. My mother was shocked to see Vaal; he was supposed to be on the road then, taking Teulin to the camp. She was given no explanation; Vaal was in and out of our flat in a matter of seconds.

I sleep in the Jasevitzes' sitting room where in the evening we play noughts and crosses or Lotto, while Aunt Katerina watches TV with the sound turned off (she's practically deaf) and winds wool. She can't remember my name and calls Boba *Boda* and Frida *Friba*.

Boba, a plum-shaped man with a sallow, reddish face, still limps from the ankle broken while he was boarding the train. He runs his household wearing an apron and gnawing a 'soother' on a ribbon: he's trying to give up smoking.

He does the shopping while I take his wife for a walk to the zoo. As a result of the accident, Frida's legs frequently give out from under her, so she clamps my elbow with such strength that in no time my whole arm goes numb.

In the afternoon it's Aunt Katerina's turn to be wheeled around the zoo. I take over from Boba, pushing her wheelchair, letting him empathise with his yak in some privacy.

Gorelko stays with his friends from the Aviation Ministry. They are important people, he says ('with the right connections'), and one can rely on their support when grappling with difficulties. 'They won't let our heads roll,' he reassures me. I hope my parents' heads – and Ararat's for that matter – can be safely counted as well . . .

It's the end of my second week in Moscow; Gorelko calls me

every day. Once when Boba and I were out shopping he popped in and left me a message with a box of apples and a pickled melon: 'Phoned your father yesterday. Ararat's back, staying in Bilibino. All done, no casualties. Sorry, didn't catch you. Going to the Caucasus. Prescribed mud baths and bed.'

Later that night we are making a list of things to do tomorrow. Boba strikes himself on the forehead; his 'soother' pops out, unstopping him.

'I forgot!' he bawls. 'I should have enrolled you in school.'

I wish he'd never remembered, but he writes at the top of the list: 'SCHOOL!' – capital letters, exclamation mark.

As soon as Boba's snoring reaches a crescendo I get up, recover my school uniform from the suitcase and push it down the rubbish shaft.

In the morning, handing tea to Boba, I direct his attention to the fact that I've forgotten to bring my school uniform with me, adding in tiptoe tones: 'So I can't go to school *now* . . .'

The same morning we head to the main department store in the city. The shoppers there queue for candlesticks, sold by weight.

'Uniforms are out of season,' we are told. 'Come next autumn.'

Boba squirms nervously and plugs himself with the 'soother'.

'Do you mind?' the sales assistant tells him with a snort. 'This is a public place.'

We come out of the Metro station: snow is in the air; a still wind. The streets are littered with footprints, filled with quiet, secret sounds. The zoo is closed. No reason given. 'I can always watch my yak from the balcony,' Boba says cheerfully.

The postwoman, lowering her eyes, shuffles down the stairs. We sort out the mail: yesterday's newspaper, a weekly magazine (weeks overdue) and two letters from my mother. Boba tells me to check the postmarks for dates to see which to read first.

I open one of the letters and read at random:

'. . . *Voluntary death is considered an honour. Chukchi custom, nothing new. They believe this is the way to be welcomed by Kele, an easy option, to make a pact with them . . . Vaal said he could take us to the place where Teulin died, maybe it's not a good idea . . .*'

I fall on something hard; it squeaks and rolls away. It's Aunt Katerina's wheelchair, parked in the corner of the corridor. I turn the page over and read from the start:

'*Did you get my last letter? Call if you want. Maybe you should talk to Gorelko. No, don't – I'll write to him later. We're packing, just a few weeks and we'll all be together again . . . Ararat's back, staying with us. She is not in good shape . . . None of us, I'm afraid, are coping well these days. About the shaman. Tumanyan thought it best to leave him with Chukchi fishermen in Uelen. He's probably still there. That's all we know. I repeat, you mustn't think Teulin died in despair. Voluntary death is considered an honour . . .*'

I rip open the other envelope, pluck the pages out. The lines are jumping, dissolving into mist.

'*Bear with me. So hard to put it into words, nevertheless it's easier to write than talk – how to explain all of this? We just heard from Vaal that Teulin is dead. It must be, I suppose, ten*

224

days since he died, almost a week before we saw you off. But of course we didn't know at the time what had happened, otherwise you would have been told. Or maybe not.

You remember that night – you were in bed when Vaal came with the meat. He said it was from Teulin, a farewell gift, rather touching we thought . . . Vaal couldn't say then that Teulin was already dead. He must have been afraid he would be blamed for his death, then detained before he could take Lel to the school.

Now he's done that he came back to tell us the truth, if not to unburden himself . . . It happened on Burnt Hill where they camped. Lel was with them. Vaal went to get some wood to build a fire. You know the Burnt Hill – there's not many trees left. When he returned Teulin was dead. Strangled. He'd tied a rope around his neck, the other end round Elgar's neck and pushed him down the slope. He couldn't fall after Elgar because he'd tied himself to a tree stump.

Lel knew what Teulin was doing, she watched him dying. She wouldn't stop him, she said. Teulin told her he was happy to go – for Vaal to have his way, to marry Lel. He couldn't help it, after all, though he'd tried, but it was no use – the tambourine, he meant, he'd lost it . . .

It's such madness! I keep asking myself, how could he? Why did he do it? Vaal's guess is that Teulin must have been scared that the Kele wouldn't leave Elgar in peace until they got their offering for the marriage. You know what Teulin thought about Elgar – he was his soul-spirit. He couldn't sit and wait for his soul to be taken away. He saved his soul by inviting himself to the land of Kele, I suppose to make a better

225

deal with them. If you can't beat them, you might just as well join them . . .

Elgar was still alive when Vaal reached him, but not for long – he wouldn't allow a deer to suffer.

I hear Boba singing the Internationale in French at the top of his lungs. It's his call for the afternoon snacks and the crosswords. Wiping my eyes, I run over the postscripts, written up the side of the last page:

'*Something else. A minor detail, compared with the rest. Teulin was a very practical man; a true Chukchi herdsman in his heart. He kept his soul intact, but he didn't want to waste what was left over. He wished us to have IT. Not Elgar – just his flesh, the meat . . .*'

I wheel myself into the kitchen, going round and round the table. Boba is scooping *meat* out of the jar – Elgar, preserved in lard. Aunt Katerina's having *him* with mustard. Frida cuts *him* into pieces, seasoning *him* with salt and pepper.

'Bon appétit!' Boba says.

We treat my parents to a trip to the zoo. Boba introduces them to his yak, who's recently been castrated for health reasons. Tata watches young stags hopping freely in the distance; a frown creases her forehead.

'Whenever I see a reindeer, I feel my stitches,' she says.

★